THE
AMATEUR
ZOOLOGIST

THE AMATEUR ZOOLOGIST

Explorations and Investigations
by Mary Dykstra

An Amateur Science Series Book
FRANKLIN WATTS
New York · Chicago · London · Toronto · Sydney

Cover illustrations
by Glenn Wolff

Interior illustrations
by Philip J. Pellicane

Photographs copyright ©:
Photo Researchers, Inc.: pp. 77 (M. W. F. Tweedie/NAS),
81 top (Syd Greenberg); Visuals Unlimited, Inc.: pp. 81
bottom (Richard Walters), 90 (Bill Johnson),
98 (John D. Cunningham).

Library of Congress Cataloging-in-Publication Data

Dykstra, Mary, 1952–
The amateur zoologist : explorations and investigations / by Mary Dykstra.
p.   cm.—(An Amateur science series book)
Includes bibliographical references (p.   ) and index.
ISBN 0-531-11162-8
1. Zoology projects—Juvenile literature.   2. Zoology—Juvenile
literature.   [1. Zoology.   2. Science projects.]   I. Title.   II. Series.
QL52.6.D95   1994
591—dc20   93-41965 CIP AC

Contents

This book is dedicated to Kathy Heidel,
who shared her love of nature with an
impressionable fourth-grader many years ago.

Acknowledgments

I wish to thank Dr. Allen Young of the Milwaukee Public Museum, who provided technical references and reviewed portions of the manuscript for scientific accuracy; Joan Jass of the Milwaukee Public Museum, who provided information on sowbugs and other isopods; Sarah Friedman and Carolyn Solie of the Milwaukee Jewish Day School staff, who shared life science textbooks and teachers' guides; the many zoologists, both amateur and professional, who field- and lab-tested the projects in this book; all of my friends, who buoyed me with their encouragement and humor; my big brothers, who let me tag along as they collected butterflies in the pasture; my parents, who allowed me to line their windowsills with rocks and feathers and other treasures; and Lucy the Cat, who provided zoological inspiration as she sat by my side.

Introduction

I was an *amateur zoologist* long before I knew what either of the words meant. As a young girl on my parents' dairy farm, I was capturing insects in the fields with my homemade net. I was caring for and learning about the cows and other domesticated animals that lived on the farm. I was discovering signs of animal activity throughout the year, like birds' nests and owl pellets and fox tracks in the snow.

A zoologist studies the many aspects and varieties of animal life. Professional zoologists have made a career of studying animals; the amateur zoologist studies animals simply because he or she finds them interesting. Your early explorations and projects, like those suggested in this book, may lead to a lifelong career in zoology.

As an amateur zoologist, I have had the opportunity to study animals in many interesting places through the years. I have banded and studied migrating birds on the east coast of the United States; I have assisted with research on orchid bees in the rain forests of Costa Rica; and I have enjoyed observing and studying animals as I have traveled through the United States, Europe, and Central America.

Most of all, however, I have enjoyed learning more about the interesting animals that share my backyard and the urban area where I now live. I can watch a colorful variety of birds at a backyard feeder, observe thatching ant colonies at work in the yard, and find fascinating arthropods living in the soil of my garden.

Part of the fun of being an amateur zoologist is that I can share my discoveries with my friends, and in turn learn more about animals from them. I have many friends who share my interest in zoology, both as a profession or as a hobby. One friend is a herpetologist who works in a museum and conducts research on tropical snakes. Another friend studies tiny flies called midges, which pollinate cacao trees in Central America. A third friend is collecting data on the butterflies of Wisconsin.

Like you, all of these people are interested in learning more about animals. All of them say that they first became interested in science—and zoology in particular—when they were in school. Each one of these zoologists has found a way to apply a strong interest in animals in a way that has made his or her life richer.

This book will introduce you to over thirty specific investigations and activities that could be used or adapted for science-fair projects. As the book guides you through these projects, it will also introduce basic techniques and procedures that can be applied in zoological investigations of your own design.

Each project is followed by questions related to the investigation or suggestions for related exploration. Think of each investigation or project as a springboard that could lead you in different and exciting directions. The possibilities are endless!

From Ant to Zebra

Scientists estimate that there are well over one million species of animals in the world. Many new species are discovered each year, and perhaps millions more remain to be identified. Each of these animals occupies a niche and plays a role within a larger habitat, where it finds the food and shelter it requires. Each animal interacts with the other living and nonliving elements of its environment. Each of these species of animals—from the ant to the zebra—has its own unique characteristics and behavior that make it interesting to study.

Yet in spite of the amazing diversity and abundance of animal life, there are certain characteristics that all animals share that distinguish them from the members of the plant kingdom. All animals get food from plants or other animals. All animals are mobile for at least some part of their lives. Animals also differ from plants in their complex tissue and organ differentiation.

The zoologists who study the many and different animals vary in as many ways as the animals themselves. Some work in laboratories, where they might study anything from microscopic organisms to the behavior of primates. Others work in the field, where their research centers on species ranging from bees to belugas (a type of whale)—and the fascinating array of animals in between. Many zoologists work in museums, where they maintain and study collections, perform research, and educate the public with exhibits and programs.

The word *zoology*, which comes from two Greek words, means the study of animals. Like other areas of scientific study, zoology itself is further divided into more specific areas. Many zoologists specialize in and study only one group of animals, just as a physician might specialize in one area of medical practice. For example, entomologists study insects, which is by far the largest group of animals. Ornithologists study birds. Herpetologists study reptiles and amphibians, and ichthyologists study fish. Other branches of zoology include mammalogy and arachnology (the study of spiders).

Biologists often specialize even more within one of these divisions of zoology. For example, a zoologist could spend his or her life studying one species or genus of fly or beetle.

Zoologists also sometimes specialize in the study of certain characteristics that many animals share. Physiologists study how animals' bodies function. Ecologists study how animals relate to other living and nonliving things in their environment. Taxonomists study the relationships that exist among the different animal groups.

WHAT'S IN A NAME?

As you read through the activities in this book, you will encounter the names of dozens of kinds of animals: arthropods, mealworms, *Daphnia*, brine shrimp, and many others. Some of these names, like housefly and earthworm, will be very familiar to you. On the other hand, names like *Daphnia* and *Hydra* may sound strange. What are all these animals, and what do their names tell us?

Each of the million-plus animals that have been identified has been given a genus and species name. This two-part scientific name is based on a system of classification developed more than two centuries ago by Carl

Linnaeus, a Swedish naturalist. Traditionally, the scientific names of animals and plants are set in italic type.

The genus and species names are usually Latin or Greek words. As with descriptive common names, like brine shrimp or housefly, the scientific name sometimes describes a feature of the organism. It may also tell about the country or place in which the organism lives, or about the scientist who first discovered or described the organism.

Knowing how and why animals are grouped and named is an important element of zoological studies. Species that are most alike in their morphology, or form and structure, are classed together in a group called a genus (the plural is *genera*). Genera that are most alike are put into a family. Similar families are grouped into an order, and similar orders are grouped into a class. Classes that are most similar are grouped into phyla (the singular is *phylum*), and similar phyla are assigned to one of the five kingdoms of living things. This book, of course, focuses on members of the animal kingdom.

An example of how this classification system works may be helpful to you. For example, you'll find that many of the activities in this book involve a group of animals called arthropods. Arthropods are invertebrates (animals without backbones) that have jointed legs and a hard, segmented exoskeleton. These animals belong to the large phylum *Arthropoda*, which includes five classes: insects, crustaceans, arachnids (including spiders), millipedes, and centipedes. In turn, each class is divided into orders, with the *Insecta* class having over twenty orders. Figure 1-1 illustrates this classification system.

You will notice that in some cases we have chosen to use the common name of an animal, like earthworm or housefly. The common name is often descriptive, telling you where the animal lives or something about the animal's characteristics.

At other times we have used the scientific name of

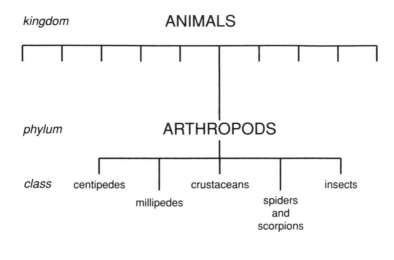

Figure 1-1. *Classification scheme of the phylum Arthropoda*

the animal, like *Daphnia*. The advantage of using scientific names is that they are universally known and agreed upon within the world's scientific community. Common names often vary from country to country, and can often be very confusing. Scientific names allow scientists around the world to use the same name for each animal.

Over time, some scientific names also become the common names for organisms, as is the case with the *Daphnia* and *Hydra*. As a result, you will sometimes see the names of these organisms in print as daphnia and hydra.

You may encounter both scientific and common names as you use taxonomic keys in field guides to identify animals. A taxonomic key is based on a series of questions a zoologist should ask to determine a specimen's identity and relationship to other organisms. You will have the opportunity to work with taxonomic keys as you attempt to identify animals in some of the following projects.

For example, you may wish to use a key featured in one of the recommended field guides (listed in the For Further Reading section of this book) to help you identify an unfamiliar insect collected in a sweep net sample. The key might start by asking how many wings the insect has; your answer would then direct you to the next step in the key. By working systematically through the questions in the key, you should be able to determine what order the insect belongs to.

A more detailed key—which may ask questions requiring very close examination of the specimen—would help you identify the family to which the insect belongs within the particular order (e.g., *Coleoptera*, the order of beetles). With practice and careful observation, you will find taxonomic keys to be very helpful in classifying and identifying a variety of organisms.

Getting Started

SCIENTIFIC METHODS

Zoologists use some form of scientific methodology to learn more about the animals they are studying. The basic procedure of questioning, testing, observing, and concluding is often referred to as the scientific method. It can be broken down into these basic steps:

1. The Problem Statement: What is it you wish to find out?
2. Hypothesis: A statement of what you think will happen.
3. Materials: A list of all required materials.
4. Procedure: The step-by-step procedure you will follow.
5. Observations/Data: A record of what happens during the experiment.
6. Results: A summary of your observations, which may include drawings and graphs.
7. Conclusion: The answer to your original problem statement. Was your hypothesis correct?

We use this basic pattern of scientific method for the investigations in this book. However, there are other ways to gather information and answer questions that are equally valid. A scientist working in a different discipline, like paleontology or astronomy, may use a variation of the scientific method described here.

GUIDELINES FOR THE AMATEUR ZOOLOGIST

1. Respect the life forms you are studying. Each organism, no matter how large or small, plays an important ecological role.
2. Follow established guidelines using *vertebrates* (animals with backbones) in science projects, such as those of the Humane Society of the United States or the International Science and Engineering Fair, which you should send away for.
3. Have a purpose for any zoological collection you make. Follow proper procedures for collecting, and carefully record data so that the collection has value to other biologists.
4. Read instructions carefully before proceeding with any project outlined in this book.
5. If you design a zoological experiment of your own, check with a knowledgeable and responsible adult before performing the experiment.
6. Keep your laboratory or work area well organized.
7. Securely store any chemicals or equipment that could be dangerous or harmful to yourself, other people, or the environment.
8. Always obtain permission before going onto private property.
9. Become aware of local laws that pertain to wild areas and the animals that live there.
10. As much as possible, leave things in nature as you find them.

TOOLS OF THE TRADE

Professional zoologists use a variety of tools to observe and study animals in the field or laboratory. You will need many of these same tools to perform the investigations that follow in this book. The equipment and apparatus you will need for a particular project will vary, ranging from simple collecting equipment like nets and garden trowels to more sophisticated apparatus like a compound microscope (Figure 2-1).

Some of the equipment you will need is specially made and will have to be purchased or borrowed. However, many of the tools required can be found in your kitchen or improvised from common household items. You will probably find that everyday objects, like plastic bags and refrigerator containers, will become an essential part of your zoologist's kit—just as they are for more experienced and professional zoologists. You will also discover that many pieces of basic apparatus, like a butterfly net or Berlese funnel, can be made using household objects and inexpensive materials. This book will give you directions on how to make some of this equipment yourself.

A list of biological supply companies is provided at the end of this book for materials that need to be purchased. These companies offer both the "hardware" needed for zoological study, as well as many different types of live and preserved zoological materials. Many of these companies will furnish a catalogue to prospective customers upon request. You might also borrow a copy of a scientific supply company catalogue from your science or biology teacher.

You will quickly notice that many of the investigations in this book require the use of a hand lens (Figure 2-2). A good hand lens is one of the most important tools a zoologist uses, whether working in the field or in a laboratory setting. Many zoologists prefer an all-

Figure 2-1. The tools of the amateur zoologist

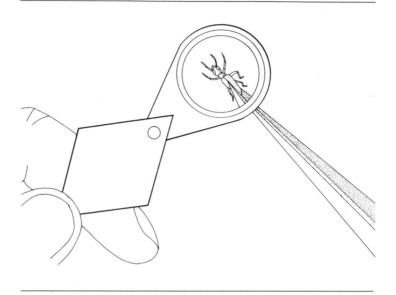

Figure 2-2. Hold your hand lens approximately 2 inches (5 cm) from your eye, with the specimen about the same distance from the lens.

purpose hand lens with a ×8 or ×10 magnification. The magnification number means that the specimen you are examining will be magnified to eight or ten times its actual size. The hand lens will help you see and identify small animals, and will also show greater detail of anatomical structures like feathers and scales.

To examine organisms even more closely, you will need to use a microscope. You are probably most familiar with the compound microscope, which is the type used by most schools or offered in home microscope kits. Compound microscopes have lenses of two or more different powers of magnification. You may have also had experience with a stereoscope, which is also called a dissecting or binocular microscope. For even better magnification, a zoologist working in a university or professional laboratory might use an electron micro-scope, which can magnify objects up to 300,000 times. The diagram and directions at the end of this chapter will help you review the basics of proper microscope use.

A variety of tools will be needed to handle small organisms in the field or lab. Forceps and tweezers will be useful in handling and examining small specimens. A camel's-hair paintbrush can also be used to transfer small or delicate organisms.

To transfer tiny aquatic organisms, you will need a pipette or eyedropper. A clear plastic drinking straw can also function as a pipette; place your finger tightly over one end of the straw and lift to suction the water and organisms.

A shallow white enamel pan is useful for finding and examining organisms. Small white plates or dishes are good for studying small organisms in the field. The white background makes it easier to study the animals with the naked eye or under a hand lens.

Collecting apparatus like nets and traps will be re-quired if you wish to capture the animals you are study-ing for a closer look or lengthier observation. Of course, you will also need storage containers like plastic bags or refrigerator boxes to hold and transport the organisms.

Other useful items for your zoological studies in-clude plastic buckets (for collecting aquatic material) and measuring equipment like thermometers, rulers, and scales.

Perhaps the most important—and overlooked—"tool" a scientist uses is a simple notebook in which to record observations (Figure 2-3). The only requirement for this notebook is that it be durable (spiral-bound notebooks are often preferred for this reason) and of an appropriate size. You may also find graph paper helpful for recording some data. Be sure to record information daily and to keep your field and lab notes up-to-date in this note-

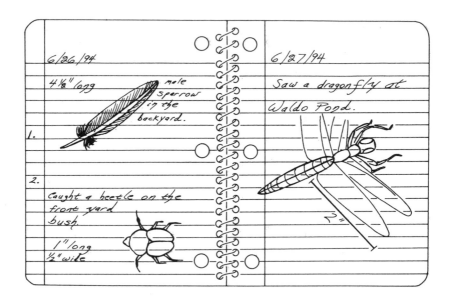

Figure 2-3. A detailed notebook is one of a zoologist's most important tools.

book. You should also include drawings and graphs whenever they prove helpful.

In addition to recording information in your notebook, it is also important to label the bags or containers holding specimens with information about where and when the organisms were collected.

Basic field guides, such as those listed in the For Further Reading section of this book, will help you identify unfamiliar animals. You can find field guides to birds, mammals, insects, reptiles, and other groups of animals in most libraries and bookstores. In addition to helping with identification, these guidebooks also provide interesting information about the animals' habitats and habits.

Other references, such as those listed in the bibliography of this book, provide useful information on specific animals and basic scientific methods. As you continue your studies in zoology, you will probably build a large reference library of your own.

Before you start any project in this book, be sure to review the list of materials that will be needed. It is helpful to assemble everything you need before getting started. If you choose to undertake an investigation on your own, or to do one of the projects listed under Further Investigations, take a few minutes to list the materials you will need.

How to Use a Compound Microscope: • Place a prepared slide on the stage, or platform, of the microscope (see Figure 2-4). Fasten the slide in place with the stage clips. Turn the nosepiece so that it lines up with the low-power objective of the eyepiece. The objective will click into place when it is aligned. Carefully turn the coarse adjustment knob until the objective is at its lowest point above the slide. Look through the eyepiece with one eye; however, try to keep both eyes open to reduce eyestrain. Adjust the mirror so that you have adequate light. Slowly raise the body tube of the microscope by turning the coarse adjustment wheel. To bring the organism into better focus, slowly turn the fine adjustment wheel until the image is clear. If the microscope you are using has several objectives, always start with the objective having the lowest magnification.

BEFORE YOU EXPLORE

With so many fascinating animals to study and so much to learn about each organism, where do you begin? How does a zoologist choose an area of research or decide what to study? And how do you choose a project from all of the interesting activities presented in this book?

A famous lepidopterist once said that he remembers

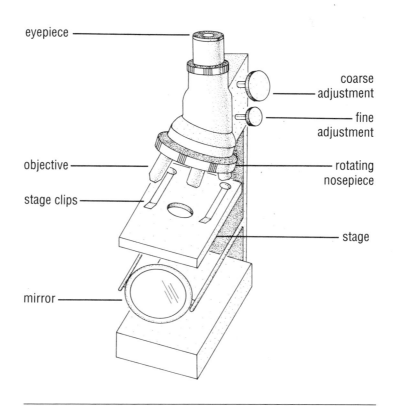

eyepiece

coarse adjustment

fine adjustment

objective

rotating nosepiece

stage clips

stage

mirror

Figure 2-4. *Parts of a compound microscope*

the exact moment when he decided to study butterflies. He saw a beautiful blue butterfly that captured his attention; he decided to learn more about it, and is still learning about butterflies some sixty years later.

Like this zoologist, you may have one particular group of animals that fascinates you most. Naturally, you might want to start with a project involving that animal. On the other hand, you might enjoy the challenge of studying an animal that you currently know little about.

In some cases, the selection of a project may be influenced by the time of year or the availability of a particular organism. For instance, it would be difficult to study earthworms or ants in the field during cold winter months.

A good way to begin any research project, however you select it, is by checking your school or local library for books or articles relating to the subject you have chosen. You should also visit any nature or science centers in your area, to see if they have exhibits or background information that will help you.

The projects in this book are organized to make each investigation interesting and easy to perform. It is important that you read through the entire investigation, from Overview to Further Investigations, before starting any of these activities. Like carefully following a recipe in a cookbook, reading all of the information is important to insure that you will be successful in performing the investigation.

The first section of each project, called the *Overview*, will give you important background information about the organism being studied, or will acquaint you with a new scientific procedure. However, remember that the Overview can only provide a small slice of information to help you get started. You will be able to learn much more by checking other sources that relate to your topic of study.

The *Materials* section, which follows the Overview, lists all the equipment and materials you will need to complete the activity. Be sure to allow enough time to gather these materials; this is especially important with pieces of apparatus, like nets, which you will make yourself, or with supplies that need to be ordered.

The *Procedure* section gives you step-by-step instructions to help you perform the investigation. It is designed to guide you through the activity or experiment as smoothly as possible. Of course, if you decide to adapt the experiment or investigation in some way, this procedure will have to be modified. It is recommended that you check with a knowledgeable and responsible adult before performing the experiment.

The section following each project, called *Further Investigations*, asks related questions and offers additional ideas for zoological exploration. Many of these supplementary investigations could also be used or adapted for science-fair projects. However, you may find that the greatest satisfaction comes from trying these follow-up projects on your own—simply because you are interested in learning more.

The projects in this book have been divided into four chapters: investigations that you do in the field, investigations that go from field to lab, projects that study live animals in a laboratory, and projects involving collections and preserved materials.

Many of the activities are quite easy, while others are more difficult and sophisticated. Some projects can be completed in a short time, while others require days or weeks of preparation, observation, and care.

With some of the experiments in the following chapters, you will be asked to make a hypothesis before starting the investigation. The hypothesis is a statement of what you think will happen. In many of these experiments, you will be introducing a variable, which may effect a change on the organisms you are studying.

In all of these explorations, you will find yourself asking questions based on what you discover. These questions can be the basis of your own further investigations, in which you gather information in an organized manner to answer these questions. If you can, locate an adult who can assist you in designing and carrying out investigations of your own design.

The appendices that follow these projects include important information for all amateur zoologists. You will find the names and addresses of biological supply companies and a list of recommended field guides. The glossary provides quick reference to unfamiliar words, and the bibliography lists other books that include information on animals and related zoological investigations.

The most important thing to keep in mind as you read through this book is that being an amateur zoologist is exciting; you never know where your exploration may lead you. So read on—and enjoy the investigations!

GUIDE TO MEASUREMENTS USED

The projects in this book use both English and metric measurements. The following chart should help you convert the measurements if necessary.

LENGTH

inch	2.54 centimeters
foot	30.00 centimeters
yard	0.90 meters
mile	1.60 kilometers

MASS

ounce	28.00 grams
pound	0.45 kilograms

VOLUME

fluid ounce	30.00 milliliters
cup	0.24 liters
pint	0.47 liters
quart	0.95 liters
gallon	3.80 liters

TEMPERATURE

To convert Fahrenheit to Celsius $(°F - 32) \times 5/9 = °C$

To convert Celsius to Fahrenheit $\dfrac{°C + 32}{5/9}$

Field Investigations and Projects

As a zoologist, the "field" you explore may be as large as a thousand-acre tract of rain forest or as small as an anthill between cracks in the sidewalk. It may be thousands of miles away in an exotic location, or as near and familiar as your own backyard.

Field studies give zoologists the opportunity to study organisms in an ecological context, as they relate to all the other things in their environment. By observing an animal in the field, a zoologist can often get a better understanding of its natural behavior and needs.

Many of us are familiar with aspects of field biology from movies and television. However, the work of a field biologist is often not as glamorous as it may at first appear. Fieldwork can be difficult, tiring, and messy. It may require working in all kinds of weather conditions, some of which may be unpleasant. However, if you are interested in animals and science and enjoy being out-of-doors, the satisfaction you will get from being a field biologist will far outweigh any difficulties you might encounter.

For the activities in this book, the term "field" refers to any investigation that is performed outdoors, whether in a field, forest, or vacant lot. The projects range from comparing sweep samples of insects to plaster casting of animal tracks, and are only a small sample of the interesting things you can study in field biology.

It is important to remember that investigations and projects that start in the field often lead to further study in a laboratory setting. The chapter that follows these field projects will introduce you to a variety of interesting activities that go from field to lab.

It often takes patience and ingenuity to find animals in the field. The following projects will introduce several techniques to help you find and collect the organisms for further study.

PROJECT 3-1: COMPARISON OF CREATURES CAPTURED IN SWEEP NET SAMPLES

Overview • Have you ever wondered how many different kinds of insects and other arthropods live in a field or forest? Zoologists use the term *diversity* when referring to the variety of species that can be found in a given area.

If you walk into a field, you may see butterflies and bees circling the flowers, and grasshoppers leaping before you. What you may not see, however, are the many insects that spend much of their lives on or near the ground. Many of these insects are most active at night, which also makes observing or studying them more difficult.

Zoologists use a piece of equipment called a sweep net to collect these insects and determine the diversity. Unlike the lightweight aerial net, used to catch butterflies, a sweep net is usually made of a heavier material like white muslin or canvas. Zoologists use sweep nets to take random samples of insects and other arthropods, like spiders, that live in tall grass or other vegetation. These nets are especially useful for collecting during summer and fall, when insects are most plentiful and active.

As the name suggests, a sweep net sweeps along the top of vegetation. To get a good sample of the resident creatures, you should repeat the sweep about twenty or thirty times in a small area. It is also good to perform sweeps both during the day and at night, to better estimate the collective population of insects.

Because different species move in different ways, it is often useful to vary the length of the sweeps you make as you move through the vegetation. You will probably have the most success catching slow-flying organisms with short, low strokes just ahead of your feet. By using wider strokes farther ahead and over the top of the weeds and grass, you will often net many faster species.

Tropical biologists frequently use sweep nets to study the rich diversity of insect populations in the understory of the rain forest. Other techniques, like fogging, are used to collect samples of insects that live in the higher levels of vegetation, like the forest canopy. This method dislodges the organisms from the vegetation above, causing them to fall onto collecting sheets or large canvas funnels positioned on the ground.

Fortunately, you don't have to travel to a tropical rain forest to find a fascinating diversity of insects. The following investigation compares sweep net samples collected from a site as near as your own backyard.

When identifying the organisms you collect, it is important to remember that insects undergo metamorphosis, and that individuals of one species can look very different during different stages of development. You may find both immature (larvae or nymphs) and adult stages of the same insect as you conduct your sweep samples. A good field guide to insects, such as those listed at the back of this book, will help you identify many of the adults as well as some of the immature forms.

In addition to insects, you may find an interesting variety of other arthropods (including spiders and other eight-legged arachnids) in your sweep sample. Although it may be difficult to classify and identify all of these arthropods, you will find the keys provided in field guides helpful in classifying and identifying many of the spiders and other organisms.

Materials

a sweep net (see Fig. 3-1)	hand lens
field guides for identification	plastic bags

Procedure

1. Select two different but adjacent habitat areas (Area A and Area B) to sample and compare. For example, you might choose a grassy lot and a forested area of the same park.
2. Prepare your hypothesis. For example, which habitat do you think will have the largest number of arthropods collected by sweep samples? Which will have the greatest diversity of organisms?
3. Collect a sweep sample of Area A. Walk through Area A at moderate speed, swinging the sweep net back and forth through the top of vegetation you are sampling. Move a slight distance to the side and repeat this procedure. Continue for a total of twenty sweeps.
4. Swing the net over your head to concentrate the animals at the bottom of the net. Grab the net to keep the insects from escaping, and transfer them to a plastic bag.
5. Examine the arthropods you have collected with a hand lens. Identify as many as possible (at least to family) with the use of a field guide.
6. Record your findings. Release the collected animals, or preserve them for further study following the techniques presented in Chapter 6.

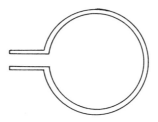

bend coat hanger to make a hoop

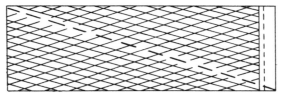

fold square piece of netting or cheesecloth once
over to make rectangle and sew across diagonal

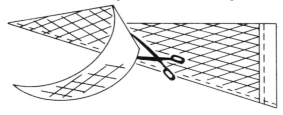

cut off excess netting or cheesecloth

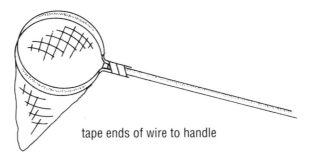

tape ends of wire to handle

Figure 3-1. *How to make a homemade collecting net*

7. Move to Area B. Repeat the procedure described above.

8. Compare your findings. Which area had the greatest number of insects or other arthropods in the sweep sample? Which had the greatest diversity? Was your hypothesis correct?

Further Investigations

1. Compare a closely mowed area of a park or yard with an adjacent area of tall grass. Does the diversity or number of organisms found vary with the length of the grass? Is there any incremental difference as the grass gets higher? (to investigate this, sweep adjacent grassy areas of staggered height).

2. Compare the same area at two different times of year. What seasonal differences do you observe?

3. Compare the same area at two different times of day. Do you see any morning-to-evening changes in activity?

4. Use a hand lens to examine the mouthparts of the arthropods collected in the two areas. Can you see any differences that relate to the food available in that habitat (e.g., seed-eaters versus grass-eaters, or chewing versus sucking mouthparts?)

5. Preserve representatives of each species collected in your sweeps following the techniques introduced in Chapter 6. Be sure to label the specimens you have collected for further study.

To make a collecting net: To make your own collecting net, you will need the following materials: a sturdy wire coat hanger (or other stiff wire approximately four feet in length), netting material about twenty-four inches square (use netting or cheesecloth for flying insects, or a heavier white muslin for sweep samples in grassy vegetation), wide electrical or duct tape, a needle and thread, and a wooden dowel or handle (like the long handle of a broom or shovel).

If using a coat hanger, you must first straighten the wire using pliers. Then bend the wire into a circle, leaving two short straight ends approximately two inches long. Hem one end of the netting to make a "sleeve" for the wire to go through. Fold the netting in half as shown in Figure 3-1.

Using long stitches, sew the bag across the diagonal to make a triangular bag. Carefully snip off the extra netting. Slowly insert the wire through the hemmed end of the net. Then securely tape the straight ends of the wire to the handle to complete your net.

PROJECT 3-2: TESTING THE RESPONSE
OF INSECTS TO COLOR

Overview • When studying zoology, it is important to remember that not all animals perceive the world in the same way that we do. You are probably aware that some animals are able to hear sounds that are outside of our range of hearing, and that many animals have a better sense of smell than the human species.

Some animals cannot perceive colors, and see the world in black and white. Other animals, however, see colors that we humans are unable to see. For example, the human eye cannot detect ultraviolet rays in the same way that many animals, including insects, can. These differences in sensory abilities and perceptions help to explain why different animals respond to different stimuli in the environment.

Insects have two large compound eyes, which may consist of thousands of tiny eyes shaped like honeycomb cells. These eyes are well adapted to detect motion. Many insects also have an extra set of three tiny eyes, called *ocelli,* which are located above the bigger compound eye.

The ocelli are sensitive to light and darkness, but are unable to perceive images or outlines.

The following project investigates the response of insects to various colors and wavelengths of light. As in any experiment, it is important to minimize other variables that might affect the outcome of your investigation. For this reason, try to collect daisy flowers that are of the same approximate size and age. If you repeat the experiment at a later date or with another type of flower, try to perform it at the same time of day and under the same weather conditions.

Materials

eight daisy flowers	masking tape
eight assorted photographic filters (including clear and ultraviolet)	aerial net
	examining jar
white cardboard	hand lens

Procedure

1. Press eight daisy flower heads (of the same size and approximate age) in a plant press or book overnight.
2. Mount each flower onto a piece of white cardboard, then cover each mount with one of the filters. Seal the edges with tape.
3. Place all of the flowers on a table or sheet in a sunny outdoor location, in an area where you know insects are regularly visiting flowers. Prepare a hypothesis: Which of the filters do you think will attract the most insects? Why?
4. Observe the response of insects. You may want to capture some of the insects to make identification easier.

5. Record and analyze your observations. Was your hypothesis correct? What do the results tell you?

Further Investigations

1. Repeat this experiment with a different kind of flower, like a rose or petunia. Do you think your results will be similar or different from what you observed with the daisies?
2. Set up an investigation to test the fragrance preferences of insects. Observe flowers in a garden or field, and identify at least four that insects (bees in particular) light upon. Pulverize the blossoms of these flowers in a food processor. Smear the powdered residue of these flowers onto 5-inch circles that you have outlined on a piece of white posterboard. Be sure to label each flower as you apply the residue. Place the board outside and observe the response of insects.

PROJECT 3-3: STUDYING ANIMAL COMMUNITIES AND POPULATIONS

Overview • Imagine that you are a census-taker. Your job is to help determine the population of a town or city or state. You might go door-to-door, down one street after another, counting the residents of the community.

Zoologists sometimes function as census-takers of a different type, as they attempt to estimate the size of an animal population in a given community. Their job is often more complicated, because the animals they are counting are frequently hidden or on the move. In addition, many of the organisms they study are tiny, making a head-count even more difficult.

Through the years, zoologists have developed several effective methods for estimating animal populations. One of the most common techniques used is the capture-recapture method. This procedure for estimating populations involves capturing, marking, and releasing animals within a chosen area.

The techniques for capturing and marking animals have been refined by zoologists through the years. You are probably familiar with some of these methods, such as those used to capture and mark birds and fish. Birds are usually captured in a mist net, and then banded with a lightweight aluminum band for identification and tracking. Fish are tagged after being captured in a hand-held or seine net. Zoologists sometimes mark mammals by clipping fur after capturing them in live traps.

Although zoologists are finding more sophisticated methods to estimate populations, such as radio-isotope marking, the capture-recapture method remains a standard technique around the world.

Population estimates are an important element of successful wildlife management. They are also important in studying environmental trends, such as the shift in the geographic distribution of a species.

For the following activity, choose any arthropod that is common in the area you are studying. You may find it advantageous to select a species that is easy to handle, like the sowbug or a type of ground beetle.

You must use a method of marking the arthropods that will not harm them, affect their behavior, or make them more vulnerable to predators (Figure 3-2). If possible, apply the paint or correction fluid to a part of the arthropod's body that is normally hidden, such as the underside of the thorax (the middle section of its body).

Materials

fine camel's-hair paintbrush

acrylic paint or
typist's correction fluid

sweep nets
(if capturing flying insects)

forceps
(if collecting ground insects)

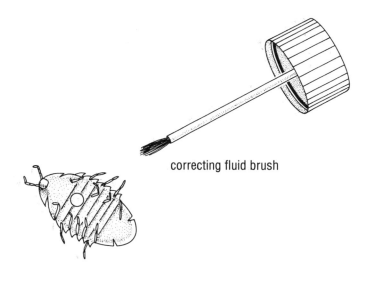

correcting fluid brush

Figure 3-2. *Carefully mark specimens to be studied by the capture-recapture method.*

Procedure

1. Choose and measure an area that you will use for your population study. The size of your study site will probably be determined by the organism you choose to study (e.g., you might choose the area under a small board if you are studying sowbugs, but would need a larger study site for a species of butterfly).

2. Collect all individuals of the chosen species that you find within the area at one time, using a net, forceps, or other method. Carefully place the organ-

isms in a plastic bag or container.

3. Carefully mark the animals with paint or correction fluid using the method described in the Overview.

4. Record the number of individuals caught and marked.

5. Release the marked arthropods at three or four spots within the area you have chosen to study.

6. Repeat step 2 of the Procedure the following day. Count and record the total number captured and the number of marked individuals within that total.

7. Calculate the size of the total population in the area by using the formula shown below.

How to Calculate the Size of a Population • You need to use a simple mathematical equation to calculate the total population. It's easier than it may look! For example, imagine that you have captured 30 beetles on the first day of your investigation. You mark these individuals and release them. The following day you capture a total 21 beetles; of the twenty-one, 10 beetles are marked.

You would record this information, and set up your equation this way:

$$\frac{\text{Total \# caught day 1}}{X} = \frac{\text{\# of marked individuals caught day 2}}{\text{total caught day 2}}$$

so

$\frac{30}{X} = \frac{10}{21}$, therefore, $10X = 21 \times 30$ or $10X = 630$ and $X = 63$.

X represents the total population of the area, which is estimated to be 63.

Further Investigations

1. Try to estimate the size of a population of animals living within a much larger area. Mark off two small sample areas of equal size (for example, one square

meter) within a field or other habitat. Calculate the population of each area using the capture-recapture method described above. Then add the two populations and divide by two to obtain an average. Multiply this average times the total number of sample-size plots within the larger area.

PROJECT 3-4: USING A PITFALL TRAP TO STUDY DAILY ACTIVITY

Overview • One of the oldest and easiest ways zoologists collect small animals in the field is with the use of a pitfall trap (Figure 3-3). The collection strategy is very simple: The zoologist buries a small container so that the top of the trap is even with the ground. The unsuspecting animal falls into the trap and is unable to escape because of the trap's smooth and slippery sides.

Zoologists often use pitfall traps to study community diversity, that is, how many different species live in a given area. Pitfall traps are also helpful in learning about seasonal activity patterns, density of animal populations, distribution of animals, and habitat preference. The investigation that follows uses pitfall traps to study the daily activity patterns of arthropods.

It is very easy to construct a pitfall trap. Simply dig a small hole with a garden trowel and sink a jar or cup into the hole so that the top is even with the surface of the ground. Fill in the soil tightly around the outside of the container. If you wish, you may place a piece of tile or wood on some stones so that this "shield" is about one inch above the mouth of the jar. A cover of this design helps to protect the trapped animals from weather and predators, and also will help attract shelter-seeking insects to your trap. However, you should still check your pitfall traps at least once a day to reduce death or predation of the animals you have collected.

If you wish to attract certain species of beetles or

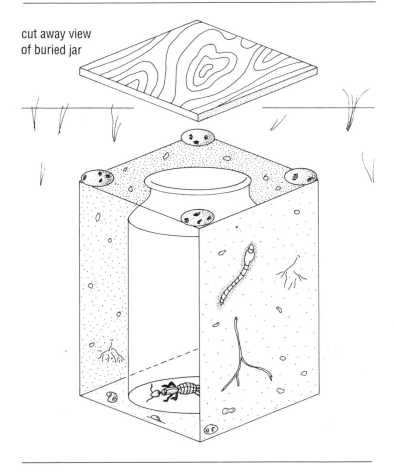

cut away view
of buried jar

Figure 3-3. A pitfall trap in position

other arthropods, it may be helpful to use a bait, such as fermented fruit or meat. The bait can be suspended over the trap or placed in the bottom of the sunken cup.

Since the environmental conditions could affect the results of this investigation, record information about the weather in your notebook at each time of collection.

Materials

garden trowel

several pitfall traps
(see Fig. 3-3)

hand lens

insect/arthropod
field guide

Procedure

1. Place several pitfall traps in an area of your choice. Position the traps at intervals of approximately twenty feet.
2. Collect the organisms captured in the traps three times daily (if possible), once early in the morning, at midday, and again before nightfall.
3. Examine and identify the organisms you have collected. If you have difficulty identifying any of these arthropods, classify them as closely as possible (for example, type of beetle). Record your results.
4. Release the organisms, or prepare them for a collection as described in Chapter 6.
5. Repeat this procedure every day for at least a week. Review your observations. Do you see any pattern in the types or numbers of organisms that are collected at different times of the day?

Further Investigations

1. Place traps in several backyard habitats such as the lawn, garden, or compost pile. Compare the types and numbers of animals collected in the different areas at regular times each day. Are there differences in daily activities between the different areas?
2. Bait several traps with meat, fruit, cheese, or other materials. Space the traps at intervals of fifteen to twenty feet. Identify and compare the animals collected in each trap. Do different baits catch different types of animals?

3. Use pitfall traps to study the effect of weather on arthropod activity. Compare the organisms collected on days that are very hot, rainy, windy, or cold.

PROJECT 3-5: USING PITFALL TRAPS TO STUDY DISPERSAL AND DISTRIBUTION

Overview • Zoologists have found that populations of animals are usually distributed in some kind of pattern within an area. For example, some species of birds space themselves and their nests evenly throughout a certain habitat.

Field biologists often study the territorial distribution of animals. An animal's territory is the area that it actively defends against other animals of its kind. Territory size varies greatly from species to species, and often varies in the same species from habitat to habitat.

Why do animals establish and defend territories? Some zoologists believe that territories allow animals to use resources like food, den or nesting sites, or courtship areas more effectively. The establishment of territories also may reduce danger from predation, as a large concentration of animals in one spot might make them "sitting ducks" for hungry predators.

The following activity uses pitfall traps and the technique of marking individual organisms to study distribution and dispersal. By charting the results of this investigation, you will be able to track the movement of individual animals.

Materials

garden trowel

hand lens

six to eight pitfall traps
(see Project 3-4)

45

fingernail polish, acrylic paint,   insect/arthropod field guide
or correction fluid

Procedure

1. Place six to eight pitfall traps in an area. Position the traps at intervals of approximately twenty feet. Mark each pitfall trap with a small dab of color or other identifying mark to help in data collection.
2. Check your traps two or three times a day, including early morning and in the evening.
3. Examine, identify, and record the organisms you have collected.
4. Continue to check your traps for several days. Review your observations, and pick a species to use for this investigation. Since this project studies animal distribution, it is best to select an animal that is abundant in the area and in your samples (e.g., a type of ground beetle).
5. Mark trapped individuals of this species with small dabs of paint, fingernail polish, or correction fluid that correlate to the trap in which they were captured (see step 1 of Procedure).
6. Release the animals where they were trapped. Repeat this procedure for several days. Record your results.
7. Chart the distribution and movement of the animals.

Further Investigations

1. Repeat this activity with one or several different arthropods. Compare your findings. Can you offer hypotheses to explain any differences you observe?
2. Conduct the investigation as described in the previous Procedure. Then introduce bait to one of the traps. How does the bait affect distribution? What

effect could the clustering of animals to the bait have on population?

3. Introduce some kind of barrier to the original study of the area (e.g., a metal sheet placed between several of the traps). How does this human disturbance change the dispersal of animals?

PROJECT 3-6: SUGARING FOR MOTHS

Overview • Zoologists use a variety of techniques, including one called sugaring, to attract and collect moths and other nocturnal insects. The method of sugaring is just what the name suggests: a sugary mixture is applied to the trunk of a tree to attract insects. The zoologist then waits until dark, and checks to see what organisms have been attracted to the sweet treat.

Light traps can also be used effectively to attract moths, since they are attracted to light as well. A simple light trap can be made by suspending a white sheet vertically in front of a lantern or other light source. As moths and other insects land on the sheet, they can be collected by hand or with an aerial net.

The following activity—sugaring for moths—will probably be most successful on a warm and cloudy summer night. However, you may be surprised to see how many moths will be drawn to the bait at other times of the year, depending on the climate where you live.

A field guide to butterflies and moths, such as those listed in the For Further Reading of this book, should help you identify most of the moths you attract. The guide will also help you review the characteristics that will help you to differentiate moths from butterflies.

The first distinction between moths and butterflies can be found in the antennae of the two groups. Unlike the antennae of butterflies, which are long and slender, the antennae of moths are rather short and feathery or fanlike. You can also differentiate moths from butterflies by noting the position of the wings while the insect is resting. Butterflies hold their wings vertically over the body while at rest; moths spread their wings sideways.

Most species of moths are nocturnal; however, there are a number of species of day-flying moths. Day-flying moths are usually more colorful than their nocturnal counterparts.

Many moths are well camouflaged and blend in with the scaly bark of different types of trees. This cryptic coloration protects the moths from predators and also makes them more difficult for us to see during our normal daily explorations. By sugaring, however, you should get a better idea of how many moths can be found living in your area.

Materials

brown sugar	paintbrush
molasses	flashlight
fruit juice	collecting equipment
maple or corn syrup	field guide to moths
bowl and spoon	or insects

Procedure

1. Prepare a mix of brown sugar, molasses, fruit juice, and syrup. Apply this mixture onto the trunk of a tree. The bait patch should be quite large to attract a larger number of insects.
2. Wait until it is dark, and then check your "sugared" tree with a flashlight. Collect any moths and other insects that have been attracted to the bait.
3. Use a field guide to identify the organisms you have collected. Record the data, and then release the organisms or prepare them for your collection as directed in Project 6-1.

Further Investigations

1. Repeat the sugaring procedure during daylight hours. Are different insects attracted to the sugar bait during the day? Were you able to collect any species of day-flying moths?
2. Test the response of moths to different kinds of bait.
3. Try attracting butterflies and other diurnal insects (those active during the day) with bait made from mashed rotten bananas.
4. Set up a light trap to attract insects. Using heavy-duty string, hang a white sheet from a tree on a cloudy night. Place a light source (like a lantern or heavy-duty flashlight) behind the sheet, and see how many insects congregate. You can experiment even more by placing light traps in two different locations: one that is heavily vegetated, and one that is not.

PROJECT 3-7: MAKING CASTS OF ANIMAL TRACKS

Overview • It is often difficult to observe animals in the field because many of them are secretive, shy, or nocturnal. However, although we may not see them moving about, these animals may be very active and mobile. Zoologists can often learn a lot about an animal's behavior and distribution by studying the tracks it leaves behind, even if the animal itself is not seen. These tracks—found in mud, snow, or sand—are clues that can tell a zoological "detective" much about the animal's daily activities.

Zoologists sometimes make plaster casts of the animal tracks they find. These casts can then be used for identification or educational purposes. The casts are also a permanent record of the footprint left behind by the animal.

You may find it easiest to find clear prints on the muddy bank of a river or stream. It is not only that animals leave the clearest tracks in the soft mud; it is also that the animals are often most abundant and active in these areas as they search for water and food. Well-defined prints can also be found in snow or wet sand.

The tracks left by the front and hind feet of an animal often differ, with the hind-feet tracks usually longer. It is important to remember that an individual's tracks will vary, depending on whether the animal is walking, running, or moving in some other manner.

The plaster cast (Figure 3-4) you will make in the following project is a reverse of the footprint found in the ground. This type of cast is sometimes referred to as a negative cast.

Materials

plaster of paris	sturdy cardboard strips
water	(about 30 cm/12 in long × 5 cm/2 in wide)
container for mixing plaster	paintbrush
paper clips	toothbrush
trowel or small shovel	

Procedure

1. Find one or several types of animal tracks to cast. Try to locate footprints that have clean, sharp outlines for casting.
2. Record information about the location of the print and the date it was found in your notebook. Add a sketch showing how the prints appeared in the mud or snow (for example, show the distance between

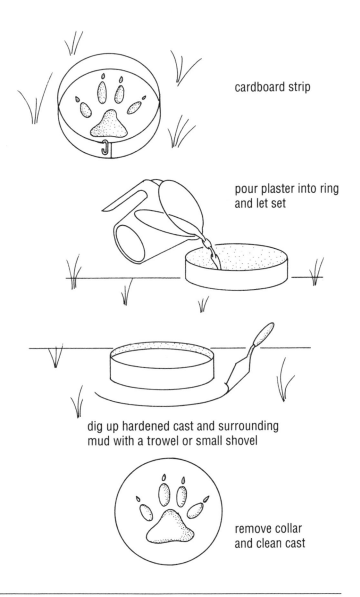

cardboard strip

pour plaster into ring and let set

dig up hardened cast and surrounding mud with a trowel or small shovel

remove collar and clean cast

Figure 3-4. *A technique for making plaster casts of animal tracks*

prints or how the prints are oriented). Give the track an identifying code (e.g., A4), and record this code on one side of a cardboard strip. You may also wish to write this code and the date in the wet plaster with the end of a paper clip.

3. Clean the area around the print with a paint-brush or stiff piece of vegetation.

4. Gently press the cardboard ring into the ground around the print. Secure the ends of the strip with a paper clip.

5. Mix plaster of paris with water until you have a creamy consistency (like thick pancake batter). Pour the plaster mix slowly inside the cardboard ring and into the print. Use enough plaster to fill the depression left by the animal's foot, and to form a layer about one inch deep above the track.

6. Let the plaster cast set and harden for about thirty minutes. Then dig up the hardened cast and surrounding mud with a trowel or small shovel.

7. Remove the cardboard collar before cleaning the cast with water and an old toothbrush. Label your cast with the date and the location of where it was found.

8. Use a field guide to help you determine what animal left the track you have cast.

Further Investigations

1. Make a positive cast of the track to show how it actually appeared in the soft mud or snow. To do this, first apply a thin coating of petroleum jelly to the negative cast you made in the previous procedure. Place a cardboard collar around the outside of the cast and secure the strip with a rubber band. Then pour freshly mixed plaster of paris into the mold. Allow this new cast to dry and set completely

before separating the negative from the positive. Wipe off any traces of petroleum jelly.

2. If you live in an area that receives snow, you will find it interesting to study and cast the tracks left in the snow. To make a cast of a footprint in snow, use a plant mister to gently coat the track with a little water. The water will freeze to form a thin coat of ice over the surface of the footprint, which helps to retain the shape of the track. Mix the plaster of paris as described below, and pour it slowly into the snowy print.

PROJECT 3-8: OBSERVING BIRDS AT A FEEDING STATION

Overview • Some of the most important contributions amateur zoologists have made are in the field of ornithology, which is the study of birds. Nonprofessional bird-watchers have played a major role in collecting data for a number of ongoing ornithological research projects, including many conducted by colleges and universities.

Thousands of amateur ornithologists have participated in a nationwide project called Project Feeder-Watch, which is coordinated by Cornell University in New York. Volunteers are asked to count birds at feeders that can be seen at once from a single window. These amateur zoologists must keep careful records for one or two consecutive days during ten two-week periods. The data they collect is then compiled, computerized, and analyzed.

In the following investigation, you, too, will observe and identify birds at a backyard feeder. This project is also designed to evaluate the preferences of different birds for different types of seed.

When trying to identify an individual bird that visits

your feeder, it will be helpful to look for any marks or behavior that distinguish the bird from others. These characteristics, commonly known as field marks, help you tell the difference between the bird you are watching and other similar species. A good field guide to birds will assist you in looking for these field marks and identifying the species you see.

There are many styles of bird feeders that can either be purchased or made at home. There are also many books that offer instructions for building birdhouses and feeders, and that give tips on how to attract backyard birds. Feeding trays, which are also called platform feeders, are perhaps the easiest type of feeder to make and also one of the most functional. The following project includes directions for making a platform feeder.

It is important to place the feeder, whatever its design, in a location where it is protected against wind, and where it is near cover like shrubs to which the birds can escape. Of course, you will also need to place the feeder where it can be easily observed for this investigation.

Keep in mind that there are many variables that could distort the results of this investigation. These variables include weather, disturbances (like the presence of people or neighborhood cats), and the feeding activity of squirrels and other rodents.

Materials

platform-style bird feeder	binoculars
two different types of birdseed	bird field guide

Procedure

1. Place your bird feeder in a "bird-friendly" location that is easy to observe. If you choose to observe a platform feeder already in use, position a wooden

divider in the middle of its tray with weatherproof glue.

2. Set up a routine for observing the birds that visit your feeding station. For example, view the bird feeder for a thirty-minute period at a specific time each day when birds are active.

3. Measure equal amounts of the two types of seeds. Pour seed A on one side of your tray, seed B on the other.

4. Observe and identify the birds that visit the feeder at your selected time. Record both the species and number of individual birds you observe at each side of the feeder.

5. At the end of the thirty-minute period, remove and measure the remaining seed from each side of the feeder. Review your findings.

Further Investigations

1. Set up an investigation to study the daily activities of birds at a feeder. Observe and record the birds that visit the feeder at least four or five times each day (e.g., early morning, mid-morning, noon, mid-afternoon, and late afternoon). Try to minimize variables in this experiment by keeping the supply and type of food constant. It will be impossible for you to control the weather, of course, but it will be important to note weather conditions in your notebook.

2. Vary the height of a platform feeder to test the response of birds.

3. Experiment with other types of feeders and seeds.

Directions for Building a Simple Platform Feeder • Select a board of a size that is appropriate for the location of your feeder. Drill several small holes in the board to provide drainage when it rains or snows (ask an adult to assist you if necessary). Using nails or weatherproof glue, attach narrow strips of wood (e.g., molding, old wooden rulers, or other scrap wood can be used) to all four sides of the board. This border will minimize the amount of seed that is blown by the wind or scattered by visiting birds. Use weatherproof glue to position a divider down the middle of the platform. Fasten the feeder to a windowsill with metal brackets, or nail it to the top of a post or tree stump.

The divider that is needed for this investigation will not disturb the general use of the feeder, whether or not it is used to separate different types of food.

From Field
to Lab

Although numerous zoology projects begin outdoors where animals are most abundant, many projects or types of research also require a laboratory setting for follow-up investigations. It is often necessary to observe the subject animal in captivity to collect additional data.

One of the advantages of doing zoological research in a lab is that it is often easier to observe an individual animal over an extended period. You are also able to set up controls that will help in collecting data. In addition, a laboratory often provides easier access to the equipment and instrumentation needed for many types of zoological study.

A zoologist's lab might be located in a university, museum, field station, or at home. You can set up and equip your own lab at home. Be sure to store carefully any materials that may be hazardous to others in your household.

If you remove animals from the wild for observation in your lab, return them to their outdoor habitat as quickly as possible after you have completed your investigation. If possible, release the organisms in the same area where they were collected. Also, try to minimize any disturbances as you return these wild animals to the field, forest, or aquatic habitat from which they came.

It is important to remember that you should release

animals to the wild only during a time of year when they can survive. For example, you would not want to release the earthworms from your wormery during the middle of winter in a northern state.

In the following projects you will learn how to collect aquatic organisms with a homemade plankton net, how to use a Berlese funnel to study arthropods, how to build "farms" for ants and earthworms, and more.

Be sure that any animals captured in the field and then observed in your laboratory are properly cared for during the time you have them in captivity.

PROJECT 4-1: COMPARING POND AND STREAM SAMPLES

Overview • Freshwater ponds and streams often support a rich diversity of animal life, ranging from a fascinating variety of microscopic organisms to the larger arthropods and vertebrates. Many factors influence the types and numbers of animals—and plants—that can be found there. These factors include water temperature, presence of pollutants, and amount of light.

In a stream, the velocity of the water current also plays a critical role, affecting both the amount of oxygen present in the water and the type of food that is available for resident animals.

To collect specimens in a pond or stream, you can use a plankton net. Plankton nets can be purchased from biological supply companies, or made at home following the directions on page 61. Simply drag the net through the water while walking along a shore or dock. Tiny aquatic animals will be captured in the vial at the top of the net, and can be brought back to the lab for identification and further study.

In order to better understand the needs of the animals you collect, you may wish to measure and record physical conditions at the collection site. These measurements could include water temperature and depth, as well as a pH reading for acidity (using litmus paper or a pH meter).

The tiny aquatic organisms that you collect can be best viewed under a microscope. You will find that the easiest way to observe microscopic aquatic animals is with a wet mount slide. With this technique, you simply place a drop of water in the center of a glass microscope slide, and then gently lower a coverslip (at approximately a 45-degree angle) on top of the drop.

You might also wish to use a depression slide, also called a concavity slide, when observing aquatic organisms. This type of slide is thicker and has a well in the middle that holds a small amount of water and the organisms. These specialized slides allow the animals to move within a limited area, and yet give the necessary flatness on top for clear viewing. Concavity slides can be purchased from most scientific supply companies.

Some zoologists recommend the following technique for preparing a hanging-drop slide (Figure 4-1). First, apply a thin layer of petroleum jelly around the cavity of the slide. Then place the drop of water (with the organism) to be examined in the middle of a coverslip. Use a tweezer to quickly invert the coverslip. Place the coverslip, with the hanging drop, over the cavity in the slide and gently press it in place to make a seal with the petroleum jelly. The jelly holds the coverslip in place while you view the slide under the microscope.

Materials

plankton or other dip net (see Figure 4-2)	slides (regular and depression)
microscope	jars or vials

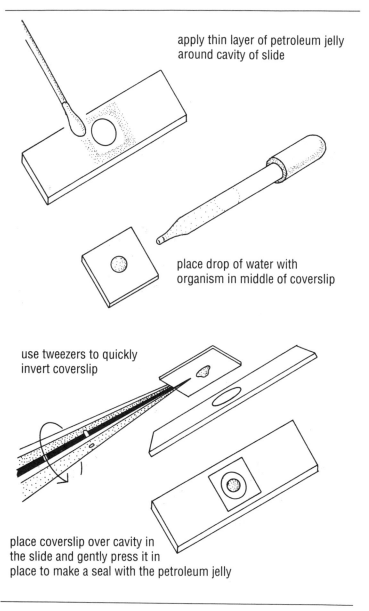

apply thin layer of petroleum jelly around cavity of slide

place drop of water with organism in middle of coverslip

use tweezers to quickly invert coverslip

place coverslip over cavity in the slide and gently press it in place to make a seal with the petroleum jelly

Figure 4-1. How to prepare a hanging-drop slide

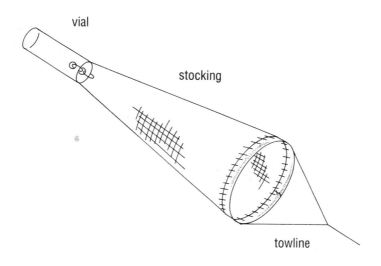

vial

stocking

towline

Figure 4-2. *A homemade plankton net for collecting aquatic organisms*

How to make a plankton net: Cut off one leg of a pair of pantyhose, and then cut off the toe. Make a ring about 8 inches (20 cm) in diameter from a wire coat hanger. Fasten the widest end of the stocking to the ring; attach a glass or plastic vial to the narrow end. Tie a towline made of fishing line to the ring on the end of the plankton net.

Procedure

1. Using a plankton net, collect a sample of water and its resident organisms from a pond. Label the sample with the date and location.
2. Use a microscope to examine your sample. With the use of a field guide to pond life (such as those listed in the For Further Reading section), identify as many organisms as you can. Record your observations.
3. Collect a second sample of water from a nearby stream. Again, label the sample for future reference.
4. Repeat step 2.
5. Compare your findings. Did you find any of the same organisms in the two samples? Which sample had the most diversity of animal life?

Further Investigations

1. Use a long-handled dip net to collect larger aquatic organisms from a pond or stream. Set up an aquatic environment for the insects and other aquatic arthropods as shown in Figure 4-3. Try to replicate the animals' natural environment as closely as possible, using water taken from the collection site. Also include plants and bottom debris from the pond or stream where the organisms were collected. If the animals were collected from a stream, it may be necessary to aerate your aquarium with an air pump. Observe and record the activity of your aquatic collection.

To make an insect aquarium: Line the bottom of a small aquarium with clean gravel or coarse sand. Slope the bottom to provide both shallow and deep areas for your organisms. Since many aquatic insects can fly, it is advisable to add a wire screen for protection.

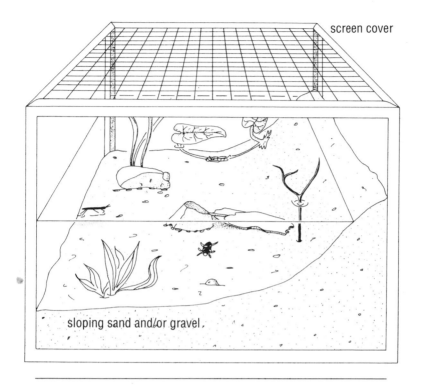

screen cover

sloping sand and/or gravel,

Figure 4-3. *Use a small glass aquarium and create your own insect aquarium to study aquatic insects.*

PROJECT 4-2: USING A BERLESE FUNNEL TO STUDY ARTHROPOD DIVERSITY

Overview • A Berlese funnel uses light and heat to drive small animals out of a substrate like leaf litter or soil and into a collecting vial. You can purchase a Berlese funnel from a biological supply company, or make one yourself using common household objects.

To make a Berlese funnel, you will need the following items: a large plastic funnel, a glass jar large enough to accommodate the funnel, and a table lamp or other

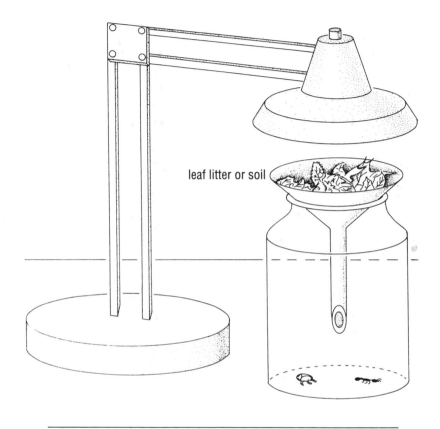

leaf litter or soil

Figure 4-4. A Berlese funnel in operation

light source (see Fig. 4-4). A plastic funnel is preferable because it creates the least condensation under the heat of the lamp.

Position the funnel in the jar so that there is room at the bottom for the organisms to exit. If you wish to keep live specimens for further observation, line the base of the jar with blotting paper or a piece of paper towel.

By using a powerful hand lens or a microscope, you

should be able to notice distinguishing characteristics in the gross morphology, or form, of the animals collected in your Berlese funnel. With the help of basic field guides to insects and other arthropods, you should be able to identify most of the organisms you collect as to order or family.

For example, you will probably find the larval or immature form of many arthropods present in the leaf litter or soil samples you collect. A majority of these tiny arthropods are arachnids, including mites, which can be identified by four pairs of walking appendages. You will also probably find different species of wingless insects, which are differentiated by three pairs of legs. A field guide will assist you in further classifying and identifying these specimens.

If you want to preserve the specimens you collect, put a 70 percent alcohol solution (seven parts alcohol to three parts distilled water) in the collecting jar. As the alcohol will evaporate under the heat of the lamp, check the level of alcohol regularly and add more as needed. If the alcohol accidentally evaporates, add a few drops of glycerine to each 100 ml of alcohol to prevent your specimens from drying out.

Preserved specimens should be carefully transferred to small tubes of alcohol for storage and further investigation. You can make tools for handling delicate specimens by gluing together pins and toothpicks. You can also use the moist tip of a small paintbrush for picking up specimens. Be sure to label each tube immediately to identify the location and date of collection.

Materials

garden trowel	large glass jar
plastic bags	table lamp or other light source
plastic funnel	hand lens or microscope

Procedure

1. Use a garden trowel to collect several samples of soil or leaf litter. Try to collect samples that are quite uniform in size, such as squares approximately 15 cm by 4 cm deep (about 6 in × 1½ in).
2. Place the samples into plastic bags and seal the bags tightly. Label each bag to record the time and location of collection. These bagged samples can be refrigerated for up to two weeks.
3. Remove one sample from its bag and allow it to dry out slightly at room temperature before placing it into the Berlese funnel.
4. Use a hand lens or microscope to examine and identify the animals you find. Record your findings.
5. Repeat steps 3 and 4 with your other sample(s).

Further Investigations

1. Collect samples of leaf litter from deciduous and coniferous forests. Record the temperature of the air and leaf litter, and any other data you feel may be pertinent (e.g., pH level). Using your Berlese funnel, extract the animals from each sample. Compare the size and composition of animal populations collected from each forest habitat.
2. Collect samples of leaf litter from the same site during different seasons or in varying weather conditions. Use your Berlese funnel to extract the animals, and compare your findings. When are the cryptozoa (the "hidden animals," or collective assembly of arthropods and other animals found in the leaf litter or soil) most abundant? Does the composition of the population vary from season to season? How do moisture conditions affect the populations?
3. Make an insect aspirator (see Figure 4-5) as an alternative way to extract arthropods from leaf litter. Aspirators are often used by zoologists to collect

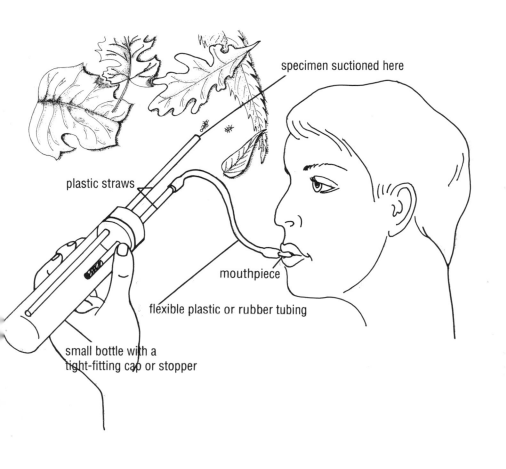

specimen suctioned here

plastic straws

mouthpiece

flexible plastic or rubber tubing

small bottle with a
tight-fitting cap or stopper

Figure 4-5. *Use an insect aspirator to capture insects and other small organisms.*

small and delicate creatures from the litter or other places. Collect a sample of leaf litter and then strain the collected material onto a clean white surface. Use your insect aspirator to suck up the creatures for identification and study.

Directions for making an insect aspirator: You will need a small bottle with a tight-fitting cap or stopper, two plastic straws, and a piece of flexible plastic or rubber tubing (Figure 4-5). Drill two holes, the size of the straws, in the cap or stopper. Insert one straw to within a centimeter of the bottom of the bottle. Insert the second straw so that about two centimeters extends into the bottle, and then cut it so that one centimeter extends above the stopper. Seal the spaces around the straw with silicone bathtub caulk. Attach one end of the tubing to the short straw, and seal the joint with caulk. Place a piece of filter or fine netting over the end of the short straw to prevent any animals from being sucked into your mouth.

PROJECT 4-3: WORMERY STUDIES

Overview • Earthworms feed on leaves and decaying animal fragments, which are recycled through the digestive process. They play an important ecological role, as they enrich the soil by pulling fresh and rotting leaves, which are on top of the ground, into the layers below. Earthworms also help to mix the soil layers, to aerate the ground, and to provide drainage as they tunnel through the soil.

The directions for making a wormery, also known as a vermicarium, are described in the following project. You could also use a very large jar, filled with alternate layers of sand and soil, if you are only keeping a small number of worms.

You will probably see numerous tunnels in your

wormery, and also notice a merging of the soil layers. You may also find wormcasts, which are made up of coils of molded soil. This undigested soil is excreted and deposited on the surface of the ground.

Earthworms have two sets of muscles, circular and longitudinal, to help them move. The alternating action of these two types of muscles helps the worm push its way through the soil. The bristly setae located on each segment of the worm's body provide traction and help the worm cling to the tunnels within its burrow.

All mature earthworms have a clitellum, or "saddle," around the middle of the body. This enlarged section is used in reproduction. Earthworms contain both male and female reproductive organs, but an earthworm cannot fertilize its own eggs.

Materials

two sheets of clear plastic	garden trowel
three-sided wooden frame	earthworms
screws and screwdriver	light-blocking cloth
soil of different types	hand lens
rotting leaves	

Procedure

1. Construct a wormery using sheets of clear plastic and a wooden frame (see Fig. 4-6).
2. Fill your wormery nearly to the top with layers of different types of soil (e.g., sand, peat, and potting soil). Pack the soil firmly and water the top. Maintain your wormery throughout this investigation by sprinkling it regularly with water (the soil must be kept damp at all times).
3. Place a few rotting leaves on top of the soil for the worms to feed on.
4. Use a garden trowel or small shovel to dig up about ten or twelve earthworms. Be sure you have permis-

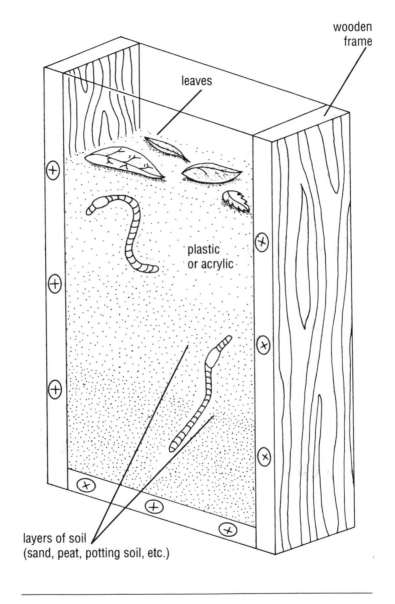

Figure 4-6. Make a vermicarium (wormery) to study earthworm life-styles.

sion to dig before collecting your study specimens. You can also purchase earthworms for this study from a fishing bait store.

5. Examine one of the earthworms with a hand lens, and record your observations. Can you find the clitellum and numerous setae (bristles that help the earthworm move)?

6. Carefully place the earthworms on top of the soil in your wormery.

7. Cover the top of the wormery with a large towel or other opaque cloth to block the light. After a few days have passed, remove the cover and inspect your wormery. Record your observations.

Further Investigations

1. Place one of the earthworms on a moist paper towel. Examine the worm with your hand lens. Locate the mouth, anus, setae, and clitellum. Make a sketch of the earthworm. Observe how the earthworm moves.

2. Try to determine the feeding preferences of your earthworms by systematically placing different kinds of leaves on the top of your wormery. Are some of the leaves pulled into the soil for food before others?

3. Investigate how earthworms respond to varying levels of dampness. Place two paper towels, one damp and one dry, side by side in a container or pan. Place a worm on the overlapping area between the two towels. Observe and record the worm's behavior.

To make a vermicarium (wormery): Attach two sheets of clear plastic or acrylic to a U-shaped wooden frame, using screws or heavy duct tape. Most references recommend dimensions of approximately 12 by 18 inches for a vermicarium. Then fill the wormery nearly to the top with layers of different types of soil. Pack the soil firmly before lightly watering the top.

PROJECT 4-4: STUDYING THE BEHAVIOR OF ANTS

Overview • Have you ever heard anyone called a "social butterfly"? Butterflies, in fact, are not social insects; however, ants and bees and wasps are. Social insects, such as ants, live in colonies that have well-defined roles and division of labor. The colonies enable the ants and other social insects to cooperate in food gathering and in the defense of their home and young. The size of an ant colony can vary from about a dozen to several thousand individuals.

The queen ant is noticeably larger than the others, perhaps two or three times their size. The queen's job is to lay eggs, which will produce new ants to keep the colony going. In fact, she is the only female in that ant colony who will lay eggs. However, other queens developing in the colony will later leave to lay eggs and start new colonies.

The queen is constantly fed and groomed by the many worker ants. The worker ants are also females, but unlike the queen are unable to lay eggs.

The third caste of ants in the colony is made up of wingless males. The only job of these wingless males is to mate with the queen and fertilize her eggs. The males die soon after mating.

The worker ants lay down scent trails as they venture out for food. These scent trails help the workers find their way back to the nest or food source. Each ant colony has its own unique odor, which helps the ants to repel intruders and to recognize members of their own colony.

You can purchase an ant farm kit, but it may be more interesting and satisfying for you to build your own formicarium, which is a home for ants (Figure 4-7). Whether it is homemade or purchased, you should keep your formicarium out of direct sunlight. It is also important to keep the soil within your formicarium moist by adding a few drops of water as needed.

Materials

two "nesting" widemouthed jars	plastic straw
trowel or large sturdy spoon	black construction paper
soil	tape
ants	lettuce, bread crumbs, and carrots
muslin or fine nylon mesh	small piece of sponge
rubber band	shallow tray

Procedure

1. Place the small glass container inside of the larger one. Fill the space between the jars with sandy soil as shown in Figure 4-7. Be sure to use soil that is free of stones or other debris. If necessary, use a small piece of clay or other adhesive to hold the jars in position before adding the soil.
2. Push the plastic straw into the soil and to the bottom of the jar.
3. Find an ant nest outdoors. Observe and record the behavior of the ants before disturbing the colony. Then carefully dig down into the nest with a spoon. Place the loose soil (and ants) into a plastic bag or coffee can. Be sure to get an assortment of adults, larvae, and pupae to stock your formicarium. If you fail to collect the queen, the rest of the colony will die within a few days.

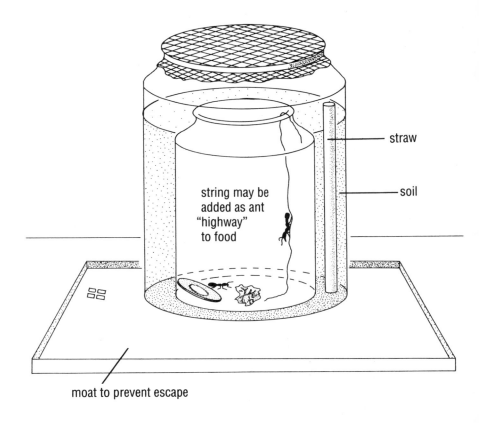

straw

soil

string may be
added as ant
"highway"
to food

moat to prevent escape

Figure 4-7. *How to make a homemade formicarium
(a domicile for ants)*

4. Place the ants in the refrigerator for about five minutes to quiet them so that they will be easier to handle. Then gently put the ants into the space between the two jars. Securely fasten a piece of muslin

or mesh over the top of the containers with a rubber band. Set the formicarium in a shallow tray of water to create a moat, which will prevent the unwanted escape of ants into your house.

5. Tape a piece of black construction paper around the outside jar. Remove the paper to observe your ant colony. Record your observations on a daily basis.

6. Place small pieces of lettuce, bread crumbs, and carrots inside the inner "feeding" jar two times a week. Remove leftover food before adding new to avoid spoilage. A small piece of moistened sponge should also be placed in the inner jar to provide water for the ants.

Further Investigations

1. Collect several ants from a different nest or anthill and add them to your colony. Mark these newcomer ants with typist's correction fluid for easy identification. Then introduce the new ants to the colony you are culturing. Observe and record the behavior of the resident ants in response to the "intruders."

2. Mark individual ants using typist's correction fluid (as described in Project 3-5). Observe and record the activities of these marked ants.

3. Study the feeding preferences of ants in the field. Find an anthill, and visualize a circle around the anthill that is about a foot from the center at all spots. Place a spoonful of tuna or cat food on the imaginary circle. Put a leaf covered with honey or syrup on the circle about one foot from the tuna or cat food. Place a spoonful of a third food, like a fruit or vegetable, on the circle about a foot from the others. Observe and record the behavior of the

ants in response to the food. Do the ants you are studying show a preference for any one of the three foods?

PROJECT 4-5: MOISTURE PREFERENCES OF SOWBUGS

Overview • The sowbug is a small brown or gray arthropod with an oval body and a distinctive carapace, or shell, that resembles the armor of an armadillo (Figure 4-8). If you examine a sowbug with a hand lens, you will notice that it has seven pairs of legs—which tells you that it is not a member of the insect order. Instead, the sowbug belongs to the order *Isopoda*, which is characterized by seven thoracic segments, each bearing a pair of walking legs.

Sowbugs are unique because they are among a small number of land crustaceans. Although sowbugs and other isopods resemble insects, they are actually most closely related to marine crustaceans like lobsters, crayfish, and crabs. Like their aquatic relatives, sowbugs breathe with the use of gills. The gills must be kept damp, so that they can absorb oxygen from the air. As a result, sowbugs are usually found in damp places, like the underside of boards or rocks or in decaying vegetation on the ground.

Some species of sowbugs exhibit interesting protective behavior. For example, sowbugs of the genus *Armadillidium* have the ability to roll into a ball when touched, giving them the other common name of pillbug. Some scientists believe that this curling action may help these sowbugs retain moisture.

Some zoologists also believe that the sowbug's antennae have special humidity receptors to help it find the damp habitat it requires. Like all crustaceans, the sowbug has two sets of antennae.

Figure 4-8. *Sowbugs are land crustaceans with seven pairs of walking legs.*

In the wild, sowbugs feed on roots, decaying organic matter, and other vegetation. Consequently, they play an important role in breaking down and recycling waste materials in the soil. After molting, the sowbug also eats its own shed skin.

To keep a colony of sowbugs for observation, first line a container or shallow dish with damp leaves and twigs. Place one or several pieces of bark in the container to provide a hiding place for your sowbugs. Carrots or other vegetables or fruit can be added as food; be sure to remove the food if it begins to mold. Moisten the container as needed to maintain a damp environment for the sowbugs.

Materials

approximately ten sowbugs

rectangular plastic food storage box

cotton

water

paintbrush (for handling sowbugs)

Procedure

1. Collect approximately ten sowbugs in the field. Remember—sowbugs are usually found in damp places, like the underside of boards or rocks.
2. Carefully place the sowbugs into the plastic container.
3. Attach a long strip of cotton to the lid of the container. Wet half the length of the cotton with water; leave the other half of the strip dry.
4. Place the lid onto the container and close the cover.
5. Remove the cover after approximately thirty minutes. Observe and record the position of the sowbugs.

Further Investigations

1. Use a hand lens to examine the sowbugs you have collected. Can you locate a brood-pouch (called a marsupium, and characterized by a swelling between the legs) on any of these individuals? The female sowbug stores eggs in this pouch, and also keeps young sowbugs in this protective pouch for several days after they hatch.

2. Place three boards (of the same size) outside in different locations to attract sowbugs and other arthropods. Note any factors, like the amount or type of leaf litter, that might affect the number and diversity of organisms that might be collected. Offer a hypothesis as to which board will have the greatest number and diversity of organisms. Check the boards at weekly intervals, gently lifting each and removing organisms with a forceps for identification. Was your hypothesis correct?

3. Estimate the population size of sowbugs in a chosen area using the techniques described in Project 3-3.

PROJECT 4-6: COLLECTING SPIDERS AND SPIDERWEBS

Overview • Although not all spiders make webs, all do produce silk in the glands located in the hind part of the body. This silk is used for wrapping eggs and as lifelines, in addition to being used in the webs made by some types of spiders.

Many spiderwebs that you will find in outdoor vegetation are made by orb-weaving spiders, which belong to the group *Araneidae*. Different kinds of webs, including those made by funnel-web spiders in and around buildings, are designed to catch different kinds of prey in different habitats.

Spiders feed mostly on insects, which they capture by a variety of methods. Because of the large number of insects they consume, spiders play very important roles in the food chains of many ecosystems. Many spiders capture their insect prey with webs, while others lie in ambush waiting to attack their prey. Still others actively chase their prey, much as a cat would chase a mouse.

Zoologists have often used spiders in experimentation, including space and drug research.

Remember that spiders may bite if they are handled and feel threatened, but the bite is usually no more serious than a mosquito bite. There are several species, however, that can cause more serious injury. These dangerous species include the black widow and brown recluse spiders (Figure 4-9). Before collecting any spider, closely observe it and attempt to identify it in the field. You may then collect the spider by directing it into a widemouthed jar, which can later be "dumped" into a larger observation chamber, such as a covered aquarium.

If possible, observe one of the species of garden spiders for the following investigation. These large orb-weaving spiders are widely distributed, quite common, and easy to identify. The web of a garden spider may be as large as several feet in diameter.

Materials

field guide to spiders	scissors
enamel spray paint (any bright color)	collecting container
white tagboard or cardboard	plastic bag or screen-covered aquarium
aerosol hair spray	

Procedure

1. Locate the web of an orb-weaving spider. Observe the activity of the spider and collect field notes for several days before proceeding with this project.

2. Use a field guide to identify the spider. **Do not attempt to complete this investigation if the spider you have found is one of several highly poisonous species.**

Figure 4-9. *The black widow and brown recluse are danger-ous spiders you should learn to identify.*

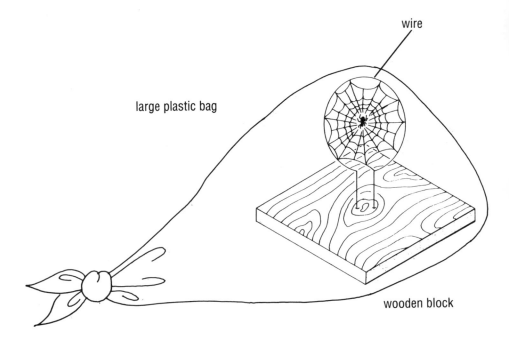

wire

large plastic bag

wooden block

Figure 4-10. *Observe spiderweb-weaving activity by building a wire spider net frame and placing it inside a plastic bag.*

3. Collect the spider for further observation in the laboratory, using the technique described in the Overview. Again, be sure that the spider you are collecting is not a black widow spider or other highly poisonous species.

4. **Following the directions on the can,** gently spray the web with aerosol paint. Then spray the web and one side of the tagboard with hair spray.

5. Quickly press the tagboard against the web.

6. If necessary, carefully cut the support strands of the web.

7. Place the spider into a screen-covered aquarium or large plastic bag, and observe its activities in captivity. Build a spider net frame with wire, and place it into the aquarium or bag with the spider (Figure 4-10). Observe and record any web-weaving activity.

Further Investigations

1. Observe and record the behavior of other kinds of spiders in the field. Can you find crab spiders, which are usually concealed on the heads of flowers? The crab spider has a large abdomen and very stout front legs. Also look for varieties of jumping spiders, which are often found on buildings.

2. Change the orientation of the net frame within the cage or bag and observe the spider's reaction.

3. Count the number of orb-weaving spiderwebs within a garden plot or other backyard area. Plot the location of these webs on a piece of graph paper. Do you see any pattern to the distribution of these spiders?

4. Remove and examine the remains of insects captured in spiderwebs. Does the location of the web or its design correlate to the type of prey captured?

Live Animal Studies in the Lab

It is often difficult to observe animals in the wild, so zoological studies are often conducted in laboratories. The laboratory setting allows a zoologist to test some things that are not easily done in the field. For example, a zoologist might test the way a crayfish responds to backgrounds of different colors. This laboratory study could help the zoologist learn more about the crayfish's adaptive mechanisms, such as protective coloration.

When you decide to keep any type of animal in captivity, you are undertaking a big responsibility. The animals you care for will depend on you for all of their needs. Therefore, it is important to learn as much as possible about the organisms and their living requirements.

As an amateur zoologist, you should always choose animals that adapt well to living in captivity. Invertebrates often make the best subjects for laboratory investigations for several reasons. They are generally easier to care for and are believed to be less subject to stress.

All uses of animals in research must be performed humanely, and with respect for the animal's living requirements. It is recommended that you review the guidelines established by organizations like the Humane Society of the United States and the International Science and Engineering Fair if your laboratory investigations involve vertebrates.

Scientists are finding many alternatives to the use of live animals in research and education. In vitro experimentation, which uses the cells and tissue of an organism, can sometimes take the place of experiments done on live animals. Computers have offered other alternatives to the use of live animals. For example, it is now possible for students to "perform" dissections with the use of computer simulations.

However, living material is still necessary for many types of zoological research. For this reason, biologists often grow living things in the laboratory, through a process called culturing. You may have read or heard of scientists raising cultures of insects, rats, bacteria, or other organisms for further study. In recent decades, zoologists have also found ways to culture animal cells and tissue outside of the organism.

Several of the projects in this chapter will give you directions on culturing animals like *Hydra, Daphnia,* and mealworms. The organisms you raise can then be used for a variety of investigations. Kits for culturing animals can also be purchased from biological supply companies, as listed in the appendix of this book.

Nine of the following projects focus on invertebrates, including several types of aquatic organisms. The last four investigations study the physiology, development, and behavior of certain vertebrates. All of these animals, from the tiny *Daphnia* to the furry gerbil, will require proper care during the course of your research.

PROJECT 5-1: THE RESPONSE OF EARTHWORMS TO DIFFERENT LIGHTWAVES

Overview • Like many other invertebrates, the earthworm is an animal with a simple brain. Its brain consists of a small cluster of nerve cells, which collect messages and transmit them throughout the earthworm's body. Each segment of the earthworm's body has smaller nerves that are in turn connected to the main nerve cord.

Although earthworms have no obvious sense organs, such as eyes or ears, they are able to respond to stimuli in their environment. Studies have shown that earthworms are sensitive to vibrations, and that they are also able to tell light from dark. Segments located near the worm's brain (in the front of its body) contain the nerves that can detect light.

The earthworms for this investigation, which studies their response to different lightwaves, can be collected and cultured as described in Project 4-3, or purchased from a scientific supply store or bait shop.

Materials

twelve earthworms	paper partitions
two flashlights	red cellophane
shoe boxes with lids	paper towels
X-acto® knife	

Procedure

1. Cut a hole (slightly smaller than the bulb end of your flashlights) in the cover of each box.
2. Tape a paper partition in place about eight inches from one end of the box. The paper should hang about 1 inch from the floor of the box, giving the worms room to crawl underneath the divider.
3. Put moist paper towels in each box (on both sides of the divider).
4. Put six earthworms onto the towels in the larger section of each box.
5. Cover the hole in one of the lids with several

layers of red cellophane. Then place a cover on each box, positioning the hole over the worms. Turn the flashlights on and place them over the holes. Leave the boxes undisturbed for about thirty minutes.

6. Remove the flashlights and box covers after thirty minutes. Observe the position of the worms, and record your observations.

Further Investigations

1. Set up an investigation to see if and how earthworms respond to vibrations. Put some earthworms on top of soil in a flowerpot. Play several notes of music. Then place the pot on a piano and play the same notes. Observe and record the worms' reactions.

2. Try to determine what part of the earthworm's body is most sensitive to light. Cover a flashlight with dark paper that has a small hole to let light shine through. Darken the room, and aim the light at the worm's tail. Slowly move the light up the worm's body to its head.

3. Set up an experiment to determine if one part of the earthworm is more sensitive to odors. Wet a cotton ball with vinegar, and hold it near various parts of the earthworm's body. Observe and record the earthworm's responses. What does this investigation tell you?

PROJECT 5-2: THE EFFECT OF TEMPERATURE ON EARTHWORM PULSATION

Overview • The earthworm has two main blood vessels: the dorsal vessel, which is above the digestive tube, and the ventral vessel, which is below the tube. Smaller vessels, including tiny capillaries, take nutrients and oxygen from these major blood vessels to other parts of the worm's body.

The dorsal blood vessel of an earthworm should be clearly visible to you through its skin. This vessel undergoes involuntary contractions, from back to front, that are important in circulating the blood inside the earthworm's body.

The following investigation studies the effect of temperature on the pulsation of the dorsal blood vessel. The earthworm you will need for this experiment can be collected outdoors or taken from a wormery, as described in Project 4-3 of this book. You can also purchase your earthworms from a scientific supply store or local bait shop.

If you find it difficult to count the pulsations of the dorsal blood vessel because your earthworm is wriggling too vigorously, you may have to restrain it gently with your fingers. If so, apply as little pressure to the earthworm as possible to avoid injury to the worm.

To conduct the following investigation, you will be placing the earthworm in shallow water of varying temperatures. It is very important that you maintain an adequate oxygen level in the water during the investigation. If you fail to properly aerate the water, it could result in death to the earthworm you are studying. Be sure to use water from aerated aquariums (tanks with functioning air pumps), and to replace about a third of the water in the culture dish with freshly aerated water about every five minutes.

Materials

earthworm

shallow dish

thermometer

ice water

watch or clock with second hand

two aquariums with pumps

water at room temperature

Procedure

1. Place an earthworm in a shallow dish, and cover the worm with water that is 22°C. Allow the worm's body to adjust to this temperature for approximately twenty minutes.
2. Observe the earthworm, and pick one spot where the dorsal blood vessel is clearly visible to you. Count the number of contractions in that spot over a three-minute period.
3. Gradually lower the temperature of the water to 12°C by adding cold water. Again, allow about twenty minutes for equilibration, and then repeat the pulsation count again. Record the results.
4. Repeat step 3, but this time lower the water temperature to 4°C. Count and record the results.
5. Return the worm to the soil in your wormery.

Further Investigations

1. Plot the findings of your experiment on a graph. Record the temperature on the horizontal axis and the pulsations per minute on the vertical axis.
2. Repeat this investigation with several other earthworms. Compare the results. Do you note any variations?

PROJECT 5-3: THE EFFECT OF CROWDING ON ADULT MILKWEED BUGS

Overview • The large milkweed bug (Oncopeltus fasciatus) is a fascinating insect that has been widely used in research (Figure 5-1). Scientists often choose this true bug for experiments since it is a fairly typical representative of its order (Hemiptera), and because it is large enough to be easily observed in laboratory settings. In addition, milkweed bugs are easy to care for because

Figure 5-1. *Adult milkweed bugs can be found feeding on the seed pods of milkweed plants.*

they require little space, have a fairly short life cycle, and are quite resistant to diseases and parasites.

You may be fortunate enough to find and collect milkweed bugs in the wild. As you might expect, the adult bugs can be found feeding on the seed pods of milkweed plants. If you are unable to find milkweed bugs in the field, you can purchase their eggs, food, and culture kits from scientific supply companies, as listed in the appendix of this book.

The milkweed bug is one type of insect that goes through incomplete metamorphosis. Incomplete metamorphosis is development in three stages: egg, nymph, and adult. The immature insects, which are called nymphs, resemble the adults. They have the same mouthparts and eat the same foods as the adult milkweed bugs. With each molt, the nymph grows in size and resembles the adult more. In addition, wings develop on the nymph's thorax, or middle section. Other insects that go through incomplete metamorphosis include grasshoppers and crickets.

The bright colors of the adult milkweed bug warn predators that it is poisonous to eat. The poisonous substance in the bug's body comes from alkaloids contained in the plants they eat, like milkweed. As with some other insects, including the monarch butterfly, the milkweed bug can safely ingest this chemical, and then absorb and store it as its own defense mechanism. As a result, the milkweed bug is usually not preyed upon by other animals.

The following investigation studies the effect of crowding on adult milkweed bugs. Since the size of the container is the variable in this experiment, try to keep all other conditions (such as the amount of food and water, exposure to light, and temperature changes) the same in the two cultures (Figure 5-2).

Materials

two glass jars or plastic refrigerator containers (one large, one small)

hand lens or microscope

adult milkweed bugs (about twenty)

milkweed seed

cotton ball in small cup

paper towel

mesh

forceps

ruler

scale (which weighs in grams)

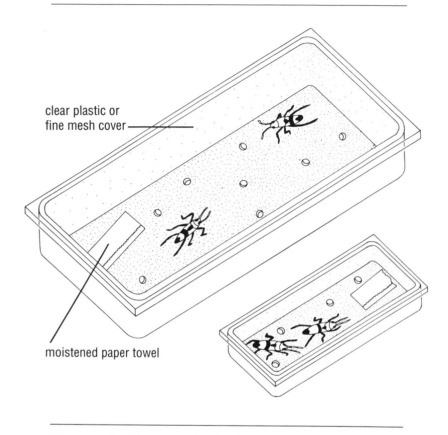

clear plastic or
fine mesh cover

moistened paper towel

Figure 5-2. *How to study the effect of crowding on adult milkweed bugs*

Procedure

1. Prepare two cultures of milkweed bugs in the storage containers, each with the same number (approximately ten) of adult bugs. The milkweed bugs in the large container will be group A. The bugs raised in the small container will be group B.

Prepare a hypothesis: What effect, if any, do you think crowding will have on the population of bugs in group B?

2. Cover each container with a clear plastic cover or fine mesh. Provide water to each group with a moistened paper towel. A cotton ball in a small cup can be positioned for the deposit of eggs.

3. Feed both groups of milkweed bugs the same amount of milkweed seeds. Be sure to remove the seeds when they become dirty or shrunken.

4. Observe and record the activities of the two cultures, including the survival rate of adult bugs. Determine an average size for adult bugs in each culture by measuring and weighing them each week. Calculate an average length and weight for groups A and B.

5. Count the number of adults in each culture on a daily basis for the duration of your investigation.

6. Analyze your observations.

Further Investigations

1. Use your hand lens to examine the external morphology of an adult milkweed bug. Try to locate the mouthparts, wings, and scent gland (located on the milkweed bug's thorax). Compare the morphology of an adult with that of a nymph. How are these two developmental stages of the same insect alike? Different? What would be the advantages of these differences?

2. Try to determine the feeding specificity of adult milkweed bugs. Experiment with other kinds of seeds, including sunflower, squash, cashews, and peanuts. Compare the development (including weight and length) of bugs fed milkweed seeds with bugs fed a different kind of seed (in an equal amount).

PROJECT 5-4: STUDYING THE FEEDING PREFERENCES OF MEALWORMS

Overview • The mealworm is the larval form of a small beetle, *Tenebrio molitor*, which is commonly known as the darkling beetle. This larva is of one of several species of small invertebrates that are very easy to keep and interesting to study in a laboratory setting.

Mealworms are readily available and inexpensive to obtain, and they are also among the easiest animals to culture in a laboratory. Since mealworms are commonly used as food for insectivorous pets like lizards, you can purchase them at most pet stores. Although this is an easy and inexpensive way to obtain mealworms for study, you may wish to raise the mealworms yourself as part of your investigation.

You can start a culture of mealworms in any well-ventilated container, like a small aquarium or plastic storage container. You will want to cover the container with a screen or other ventilated lid to keep the adult beetles from escaping.

Put a layer of bran, flour, uncooked oatmeal, dry bread, or a mixture of these on the bottom of your container. To provide moisture for your mealworms, place a fresh piece of apple or potato into the container several times a week. Remove any leftover pieces to prevent spoilage.

The darkling beetle is an insect that undergoes complete metamorphosis, unlike the milkweed bug described in the previous investigation. An adult female lays eggs, which hatch into mealworms in approximately a week. The mealworm itself, which is the larval stage, takes about six months to mature before becoming a pupa. The adult emerges from the pupa several weeks later.

The following investigation studies the effect of different types of food on mealworm development (Figure 5-3). To minimize the effect of other variables on this investigation, equalize the weight of the apple or potato piece put into each container.

Materials

four large plastic refrigerator storage boxes

forty mealworms

hand lens

bran

flour (both bleached white and unbleached whole wheat)

uncooked oatmeal

scale (which measures in grams)

Procedure

1. Prepare four mealworm cultures as follows: A—bran; B—bleached white flour; C—unbleached whole-wheat flour; and D—uncooked oatmeal. Be sure to put the same amount of grain into the bottom of each container.
2. Place ten mealworms in each culture.
3. Weigh each larva in group A. Add and average the weights to determine an approximate average weight for group A. Repeat with groups B, C, and D. Repeat this measurement at least once a week for several weeks.
4. Count and record the numbers of adults, larvae, and pupae in all four groups each day. Record any differences you observe in the four groups.

Further Investigations

1. Study the effects of caffeine on mealworm development. Feed one group of mealworms food that has been moistened with a coffee solution (about four

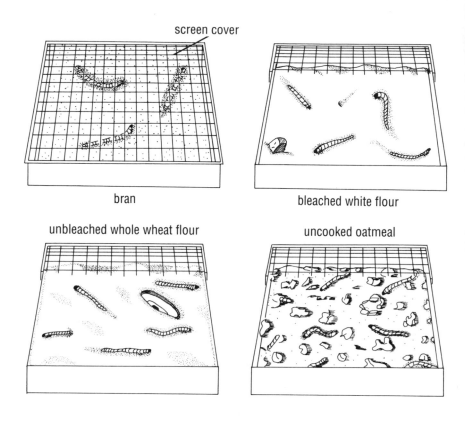

screen cover

bran

bleached white flour

unbleached whole wheat flour

uncooked oatmeal

Figure 5-3. *Experimental setup for a study of the effect of different types of food on mealworm development*

ounces of water mixed with two teaspoons regular instant coffee). Compare the development and size of individuals in this group with a control group that is not given the caffeine supplement.

2. Test the effect of various periods of light and dark on the development of mealworms. Drape one culture of mealworms (with approximately ten mealworms) with a dark cloth for eighteen hours each

day. Leave a second culture containing the same number of mealworms undraped, and exposed to normal household or lab light.

PROJECT 5-5: THE EFFECT OF DRUGS ON *DAPHNIA* HEARTBEAT

Overview • The *Daphnia* is a common microscopic animal that is also known as the water flea (Figure 5-4). It is a freshwater arthropod that is commonly found in ponds and lakes.

Researchers often use *Daphnia* in experiments because it is abundant and easy to find and collect. In addition, *Daphnia* requires minimal care and has unique behavioral and anatomical features.

Perhaps the most unusual physical feature is the *Daphnia*'s transparent shell, which is called a *carapace*. This transparent exoskeleton allows zoologists to observe internal functions, such as heartbeat. The carapace of this tiny crustacean encloses its entire body, except for the head and antennae.

It is easy to spot the tiny *Daphnia* in a sample of pond or lake water, sometimes even without the aid of a hand lens or microscope. How can you pick it out from the other organisms in the water? Just look for the *Daphnia*'s characteristic flealike movements as it appears to jump forward in the water. It uses its large and powerful antennae as oars as it propels itself quickly through the water.

Although tiny, the *Daphnia* is an important part of aquatic food chains.

As a filter-feeder, it strains small pieces of debris, algae, and bacteria from the water. In turn, the *Daphnia* is eaten by many species of freshwater fish.

You can culture *Daphnia* in a small covered aquarium filled with filtered pond water. Add distilled water

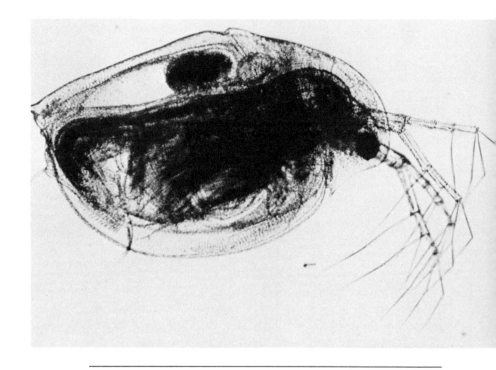

Figure 5-4. *The* Daphnia, *or water flea, is a freshwater arthropod that is an important part of aquatic food chains.*

as needed when the water level drops due to evaporation. *Daphnia* culture kits are also available from most biological supply companies.

Like all other arthropods, the *Daphnia*'s growth occurs immediately following molt. A special gland produces new shell material. The new carapace, which follows each molt, is soft and allows the *Daphnia* to grow. Under optimum conditions, *Daphnia* can live at least one hundred days.

Materials

Daphnia culture   dropper

glass slide

microscope

aged tap water

dilute solutions of
coffee, cola, ethyl
alcohol, and nicotine

Procedure

1. Prepare dilute solutions as follows: A—brew weak caffeinated coffee; B—add one part water to one part cola; C—add 2 mL of ethyl alcohol to 98 mL of water; D—soak a nonfiltered cigarette in 100 mL of water for one hour, then strain the solution.
2. Use a dropper to place a single *Daphnia* on a slide.
3. Position the slide under the microscope. Count the number of times the *Daphnia*'s heart beats in one minute. Record your observations.
4. Add two drops of drug solution A. Count the heartbeat again. Record your observations.
5. Remove the solution with a dropper. Flush the slide with aged tap water (which has been left standing overnight).
6. Repeat steps 2 through 5 with each of the other drug solutions. Chart and compare your results.

Further Investigations

1. Does the strength of coffee affect *Daphnia* heartbeat? Repeat steps 2 through 5 with varying strengths of coffee. What do you observe?
2. Study the effect of temperature on *Daphnia* heartbeat. Determine the "normal" heartbeat of a *Daphnia* in culture water (which should be about 70°F/21°C). Draw off the water with a pipette or dropper. Then add distilled water that is between 0 and 5°C. Count the heartbeat at every 3° rise in temperature as you allow the water to warm to room temperature. If you wish, use a heat lamp to warm the water slowly.

PROJECT 5-6: THE EFFECT OF LIGHT ON *DAPHNIA* BEHAVIOR

Overview • The *Daphnia*, or water flea, was introduced to you in Project 5-5. It is a common microscopic animal found in freshwater ponds and lakes. The *Daphnia*'s transparent carapace and interesting behavior make it a very fascinating organism to study.

One of the first things you notice when examining a *Daphnia* with a hand lens or microscope is its large eye. This large compound eye is made up of over twenty lenses. Zoologists have found that the *Daphnia*'s compound eye is sensitive to changes in light intensity and location. Its smaller simple eye, called an ocellus, is sensitive to ultraviolet light.

The following investigation studies the effect of light on the *Daphnia*'s behavior and orientation. Orientation refers to the way in which animals position themselves within their environment in response to a stimulus. The stimulus could be temperature, vibration, amount and type of light, or presence of a predator. This project uses the intensity of light as the variable in the experiment.

Materials

1-liter cylinder	pipette
Daphnia culture	light source

Procedure

1. Put several *Daphnia* into a 1-liter cylinder. Place the cylinder in a dark place, like a cabinet or closet.
2. Position a dim light over the cylinder (the intensity of the light, from dim to bright, can be varied by moving the light source farther away from or closer to the cylinder).

3. Observe and record the position of the *Daphnia* after they have had ten minutes to orient themselves.

4. Increase the light intensity by moving the light closer to the cylinder.

5. As in step 3, observe and record the position and behavior of the *Daphnia* after ten minutes.

Further Investigations

1. Study the effect of varying wavelengths of light on *Daphnia* behavior. Place a red filter between the light source and the cylinder of water containing the *Daphnia*. Observe and record the behavior of the *Daphnia*. Remove the red filter, and in its place position a blue filter. Do you observe any behavioral change?

2. Study the population growth of *Daphnia* as it relates to light intensity or quality (fluorescent versus incandescent bulbs, or light of different wavelengths as passed through filters). Start several cultures of *Daphnia* with the same number of adults. Make population counts every two days (removing dead animals as you do so).

PROJECT 5-7: THE EFFECT OF TEMPERATURE ON BRINE SHRIMP EGGS

Overview • Although sometimes called a "sea monkey," the tiny brine shrimp is actually a crustacean, like a lobster or crab. Brine shrimp are now found in salty lakes and puddles, but zoologists believe that they evolved from freshwater crustaceans.

Brine shrimp eggs are often purchased by tropical fish owners, who in turn raise the shrimp as live food for their pets. Many of the brine shrimp eggs found in pet stores come from the Great Salt Lake in Utah, where they are abundant. They can also be found in dry areas of the American Southwest, where ponds and puddles dry up for much of the year. The adult shrimp die under these conditions, but the eggs survive until the next rainfall when they will hatch.

It is the remarkable ability of the brine shrimp's egg to survive extreme temperatures that makes it so fascinating to study. For the following investigation, you can purchase brine shrimp eggs from a pet store or from a biological supply company.

It is easy to start your own culture of brine shrimp. If you purchase the eggs from a biological supply company, simply follow the directions provided for care. Under proper conditions, the eggs will hatch within several days.

Materials

brine shrimp eggs	dry yeast
hand lens	freezer
large widemouthed jars	oven
"aged" tap water	aluminum foil or
sea salt	ovenproof plate

Procedure

1. Mix a tablespoon of sea salt with a large jar or glassful of tap water that has sat uncovered for at least a day to dechlorinate. Pour this salty, or briny, solution into a large widemouthed jar.
2. Sprinkle a pinchful of brine shrimp eggs onto the surface of the brine.
3. Place the jar in a warm location, and check it daily. Record your observations.
4. Put a second group of brine shrimp eggs in the

freezer for several days. Remove the eggs from the freezer and repeat steps 1–3.

5. Put another experimental group of eggs in an oven for a few hours at a low temperature (about 150°F). Remove the eggs from the oven and repeat steps 1–3.

Further Investigations

1. Set up an experiment to see if the level of salt concentration in the water affects the development of brine shrimp. Prepare a control culture of brine as described in step 1 of the previous procedure, using one tablespoon of sea salt. Double the amount of sea salt in a second solution (in an equal amount of water), and observe and compare your two brine shrimp cultures.

2. Try culturing fairy shrimp, a freshwater relative of the brine shrimp, by collecting some soil from a dried-up temporary pond or puddle. Place the soil into an aquarium with rainwater. Within several weeks you may observe the activity of fairy shrimp. Since fairy shrimp require cold water, you may need to keep them refrigerated after the eggs hatch. How are the morphology and behavior of the fairy shrimp like brine shrimp? How are they different?

3. Examine the brine shrimp's digestive system. Add a drop of food coloring to the yeast before feeding a few of your brine shrimp. Can you see the digestive system?

PROJECT 5-8: TESTING THE SMELLING SENSITIVITY OF HOUSEFLIES

Overview • Many insects have chemically sensitive hairs, called setae, which help them smell, locate, and taste food. The setae are often concentrated on the *tarsi*,

103

or feet, of the insect. These receptors function in a way that is similar to the action of taste buds in your mouth.

You have probably observed houseflies "sampling" the air around them as they wiggle these setae. Just as your nose may lead you to freshly baked chocolate-chip cookies, the fly's setae help it locate food within its environment.

Different setae on the fly's body have different receptors—some for sugars, some for salts, and many others for other substances. The following investigation tests a housefly's response to a sugary solution. When the housefly extends its proboscis, or feeding tube, toward the solution it is considered a positive response.

Houseflies belong to the order *Diptera*, which includes all true flies with only one pair of wings. This group also includes mosquitoes, midges, and gnats.

Materials

sugar-water solutions (see step 2 of Procedure)	double-backed adhesive tape
	wooden dowel or new pencil
a housefly	
	hand lens

Procedure

1. Capture a housefly, using bait if necessary. Keep the fly in a ventilated jar or container for a day or two before continuing your experiment, so that the fly builds up an appetite.

2. Prepare solutions of sugar-water as follows: A— mix 5 grams of sugar in 90 ml of water. The other solutions (B, C, D, and so on) will have increased amounts of sugar in 5-gram increments.

3. Put a small square of double-backed tape onto the end of the wooden dowel or pencil. Gently touch the tape to the back of the fly, so that the fly can be picked up and moved with the dowel.

4. Using the dowel as a handle, hold the fly about 5 to 6 mm away from the sugar-water solution A.
5. Repeat step 4 with increasingly concentrated solutions. Record your observations.

Further Investigations

1. Use your hand lens to examine the housefly's mouthparts. How do these mouthparts seem well adapted for the food the housefly eats?
2. Test and compare the response of a housefly to different "sugary" substances (e.g., molasses, fruit juice, maple syrup).

PROJECT 5-9: *HYDRA* STUDY

Overview • The *Hydra* is a soft, transparent animal that lives in ponds and streams (Figure 5-5). *Hydra* belong to one of the three major groups of coelenterates. A coelenterate is an invertebrate that has two tissue layers, ectoderm and endoderm, and a large central body cavity. In addition to the *Hydra*, the other groups of coelenterates are jellyfish and a group with corals and sea anemones.

Most coelenterates live in the salty water of the ocean. The *Hydra* is one of a small number of freshwater coelenterates. You can probably find *Hydra* living in ponds, pools, and slow-moving streams in your area. Hydra are active year-round, and can even be found in winter under the ice of a pond.

Hydra appear motionless and usually remain attached to underwater plant stems and leaves. However, like other animals, they are able to move to find more favorable environments.

A single mouth opening, which is surrounded by a ring of tentacles, leads to the *Hydra*'s central body cavity. The wormlike tentacles have stinging capsules, which

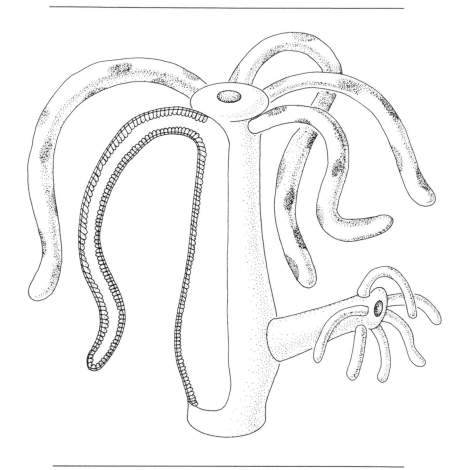

Figure 5-5. *The* Hydra *is one of the few freshwater coelenterates.*

are used to immobilize prey. The *Hydra*'s tentacles are also used for feeding, movement, and defense.

Most *Hydra* are only a few millimeters in length, and will need to be viewed with a microscope or hand lens. You will find it interesting to observe the *Hydra*'s response to touch or to the presence of food. The *Hydra* has a system of simple nerve fibers, which are distrib-

106

uted throughout its body. As a result, it is very sensitive to touch and to other environmental changes.

The *Hydra* reproduces by budding, which is a form of asexual reproduction. The bud, or group of cells, breaks off the parent when it grows to a certain size. The cells then become a new and independent *Hydra*.

To start a culture of *Hydra*, collect some aquatic plants or fallen leaves from a shallow lake or slow-moving stream. At the same time, take water from the site of collection. Place the plants with the collected water in a white enamel tray, and place the tray in a sunny (but not hot) indoor location.

You should be able to observe *Hydra* on the surface of the water and sides of the container within an hour. Use a dropper to transfer the *Hydra* to a jar filled with pond water. *Hydra* can also be obtained from a biological supply house, as listed in the appendix. Feed your *Hydra* culture *Daphnia* or newly hatched fairy shrimp.

Materials

dropper	hand lens
Hydra culture	toothpick or probe
petri dish	

Procedure

1. Use the dropper to transfer a single *Hydra* from the *Hydra* culture to a petri dish. Add enough aquarium water to cover the *Hydra*.
2. Examine the *Hydra* with a hand lens. Locate the mouth, tentacles, and ectoderm tissue.
3. As you observe the *Hydra* with the hand lens, use a toothpick or probe to gently touch the animal in two or three different places. Record the *Hydra*'s response to each touch.
4. Return the *Hydra* to the culture.

Further Investigations

1. Repeat the activity with *Hydra* that have been cooled in the refrigerator for several hours. Does temperature affect the activity of the *Hydra?*
2. Use a dropper to add one drop of vinegar to the water in the petri dish. Observe and record the *Hydra's* response to the vinegar.
3. Observe the feeding habits of the *Hydra.* Transfer some of the *Hydra* from your culture to a jar filled with pond water. Feed *Daphnia* or newly hatched fairy or brine shrimp (which have been rinsed to remove any salt) to the *Hydra.* Repeat this activity with fish food. Do the *Hydra* show a preference for any type of food?
4. Shine a flashlight on a petri dish containing *Hydra.* Observe and record how the *Hydra* respond to the light.
5. Gently tap the edge of the petri dish containing the *Hydra* with a pencil. Do the *Hydra* respond to this vibration?

PROJECT 5-10: THE EFFECT OF TEMPERATURE ON FISH RESPIRATION

Overview • As a fish swims or gulps, it takes in oxygen-rich water, which is passed over the gills. The gills, which are located under the flaps of skin behind the eyes, are made up of tissue containing many blood vessels. These blood vessels take in oxygen from the water; at the same time they release carbon dioxide into the blood. This process of taking in oxygen and expelling carbon dioxide is called respiration.

Fish are cold-blooded, or ectothermic, vertebrates. Their body temperatures change with the temperature of the surroundings. As with many other types of cold-blooded animals, the activity level of some fish drops with a decrease in temperature.

In this experiment, you will be testing the effect of temperature on goldfish respiration.

Materials

goldfish

aquarium water

250-mL beaker (or any glass jar of similar size)

watch or clock with second hand

1,000-mL beaker (or any glass container of similar size)

thermometer

crushed ice in cold water

Procedure

1. Review guidelines of the Humane Society of the United States or the International Science and Engineering Fair for experimentation involving vertebrates.

2. Place a goldfish in aquarium water that has been poured into the small beaker or jar. Then place this small beaker inside the larger 1,000-mL beaker or glass container.

3. Put a thermometer in the beaker that holds the goldfish. Read and record the temperature of the water.

4. Observe the goldfish. Count the number of times the gill cover opens and closes (or beats) in one minute. Record this count as the respiration rate of the fish.

5. Place the ice-water mixture into the large beaker so that this colder water surrounds the outside of the small beaker. Watch the thermometer. Each time the water temperature drops 3°C, count and record the number of gill-cover beats per minute. Be sure

to record the corresponding temperature and any changes in behavior you observe.

6. Continue with this procedure until the temperature reaches 10°C.

7. Remove the small beaker or jar, and pour the ice water out of the large beaker. Put the small beaker back inside the larger one.

8. Gradually pour warm water into the large beaker. Each time the temperature increases 3°C, count and record the gill-cover beats per minute and the corresponding temperature. Stop adding warm water when the temperature of the water in the small beaker reaches 30°C.

9. Analyze the results of the experiment.

Further Investigations

1. Graph the data you collected in the previous investigation. Your independent variable (the condition controlled by the experimenter) will be the water temperature, with the dependent variable the number of gulps per minute.

2. Repeat this experiment with other variables. Does the amount of light affect fish respiration rate? Does respiration vary with the type or volume of music played?

PROJECT 5-11: THE EFFECT OF TEMPERATURE ON FROG DEVELOPMENT

Overview • One of the most fascinating zoological projects is to observe the metamorphosis of a frog from egg to adult. The female frog lays eggs, which are fertilized externally in the water. The eggs hatch into tadpoles, which is the larval form of the frog. These tadpoles have gills and a long tail, which disappear after weeks or months. The final phase of metamorphosis involves the development of lungs and two pairs of legs.

In all, it takes about four months for the egg to develop into a small frog. The amount of time varies according to environmental conditions, such as temperature and water quality.

You can find frog eggs, also called spawn, in ponds in early spring as soon as the weather starts to warm. You will recognize the eggs by their distinctive appearance: a mass of hundreds or thousands of eggs clumped together in a cloudy jelly.

If you collect frog eggs yourself for this project, take only a small amount (equivalent to about a handful) and leave the remainder undisturbed. Place the eggs you have netted into a reasonably large container with pond water and a few pond plants. The pond plants will provide shelter and food for the newly hatched tadpoles, and will also release oxygen needed by the developing eggs. If you are unable to find the eggs yourself, you could purchase some from most biological supply companies.

Some of the eggs that you collect and observe may turn gray and fail to change shape. These eggs are probably infertile, or they may fail to hatch due to lack of oxygen or some other environmental factor.

Young tadpoles are vegetarians, and will feed on algae in the pond water. If you were not successful in collecting pond plants with the eggs, you can substitute a small piece of boiled spinach or lettuce. As the tadpoles grow larger and start to develop legs, their dietary needs will change. You can then feed them small amounts of finely chopped meat or small insects.

The following project investigates the effect of temperature on the development of frog eggs. By keeping eggs in two containers, one inside and one outdoors, you can easily compare development rates under different conditions. You may wish to take and record the temperature of the water in each container (at the same time each day) to help you in interpreting the results of this investigation. You should understand that the warmer the water is, the less oxygen it can hold. Do you think this fact may affect the results of your experiment?

Materials

long-handled net	pond water
plastic bag, pail, or other container (to transport the eggs and water)	pond plants
	two aquariums, jars, or pans
frog eggs	

Procedure

1. Review guidelines for vertebrate projects (such as those of the International Science and Engineering Fair).
2. Using a net or pail, collect a small mass (equivalent to a handful) of frog eggs from a pond. Put the eggs into a container that you have filled with pond water and several small pond plants.
3. After returning to your home or lab, put the pond water into two jars, pans, or other containers.
4. Divide the eggs equally into the two jars. Place one of the jars outside in a safe location. Keep the second jar inside at room temperature (and away from direct sunlight and radiators).
5. Check the eggs or tadpoles daily, and record your observations.
6. Return the tadpoles to the pond where you collected the eggs. If you purchased the eggs from a biological supplier, you may want to check with a nearby nature center to learn about appropriate release sites.

Further Investigations

1. Use a hand lens to examine one of the frog eggs. The white portion of the egg provides food for the developing tadpole.
2. Observe the behavior of the newly hatched tadpoles. Can you observe any difference in the activity of the indoor and outdoor tadpoles? Does temperature seem to affect the activity level of the tadpoles?

PROJECT 5-12: STUDYING THE DAILY FOOD CONSUMPTION OF A GERBIL

Overview • Although gerbils are very common pets today, they were virtually unheard of in our country a generation or two ago. Gerbils were first introduced to the United States about forty years ago, and have only gained widespread popularity during the past twenty years. The "pioneer" gerbils who arrived here in the 1950s were not imported as pets; rather, they were brought to America by a zoologist who was using the small rodents for research.

The following project studies the daily food consumption of a gerbil. In the wild, gerbils are vegetarians and eat a variety of plants and seed. In homes and laboratories, however, gerbils are usually fed commercially prepared rodent food. These nutritionally balanced pellets are available in most pet stores and supermarkets.

A small glass aquarium can be used as a cage for the gerbil you are observing. Cover the tank securely with a screen or wire mesh. Place a layer of litter, such as wood shavings or commercial gerbil bedding, into the bottom of the cage. The gerbil will further shred this material to make a cozy nest. Provide water in a water bottle with a metal spout.

You should clean the gerbil's cage thoroughly before starting this experiment to be sure that all leftover food has been removed. Throughout the course of this investigation, feed and care for the gerbil as you would normally do so.

Materials

gerbil
(in proper cage)

gerbil food

scale

Procedure

1. Review guidelines for vertebrate projects.
2. Weigh the amount of food you give to the gerbil on the first day of your investigation. Place the food into the gerbil's cage as you routinely do.
3. At the same time the following day, remove any food remaining in the cage. You will have to hunt in the litter for any food that has been scattered or hidden. Weigh and record the amount of food that is left over.
4. Repeat this procedure every day for a week. Analyze your results. Did the gerbil eat the same amount of food each day?

Further Investigations

1. Set up an experiment to determine if other variables will affect the amount of food eaten by the gerbil. Does the amount of food consumed vary with exposure to different levels of light or sound?
2. Investigate the daily activity patterns of your gerbil. Does it eat more—or only—at certain times of day or night?

3. Set up an experiment to test food preferences of your gerbil. Determine the daily consumption of commercial gerbil food as described above for a one-week period. Then substitute different types of food. Was there any significant difference in the amount of food consumed?

PROJECT 5-13: CONDITIONED RESPONSES IN RATS

Overview • The white rat has been used extensively in lab experiments to study everything from nutrition to conditioned responses. White rats have helped zoologists learn about dietary needs, disease control, intelligence, and much more.

Through research, zoologists have learned that some animals can be trained to perform complex tasks by rewarding them for certain behavior. By providing positive reinforcement, the animal is conditioned to behave in a certain way.

In the following investigation, the rat is given food as a reward for successfully going through the maze. The experiment studies the behavior of the rat in response to this positive reinforcement.

Because all species of rats reproduce quickly and often, it is best to house male and female rats separately. Females can give birth to their first litter when they are less than three months old. The females of that litter, in turn, can be breeding within two more months. It is estimated that a single pair of rats could multiply to a colony of over fifty thousand within one year if all the offspring survived.

White rats are usually quite easy to handle; however, always handle a rat very carefully to avoid injury to either yourself or to the animal you are studying. If you need to pick up the rat to transfer it to the maze, lay the palm of your hand across its back and put your thumb and forefinger under its chin. Then carefully support the rat's body with your other hand.

Materials

white rat

rat food

stopwatch (or other watch with a second hand)

cardboard or wooden maze

Procedure

1. Review guidelines for vertebrate projects.
2. Construct a maze similar to the one illustrated in Figure 5-6.
3. Place a food reward at the end of the maze.
4. Carefully transfer the rat from its cage to the entrance of the maze. Time the rat as it wanders through the maze for the first time. Record how long it took the rat to get from the entrance to the reward at the other end.
5. Repeat this procedure for several days, always using the same rat. Record the time, and note any changes in the rat's behavior as it moves through the maze.

Further Investigations

1. Repeat this activity with a different rat. Compare the results. Do you think that all rats learn at the same rate?
2. Experiment with other conditioned responses. For example, can you train a rat or other animal to respond to a sound, like the ringing of a bell?
3. Line the bottom of a large box or other container with a sheet of paper ruled with 4-inch squares.

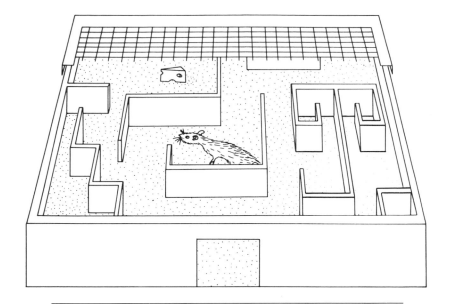

Figure 5-6. *Design your own maze to study conditioned responses in rats (Project 5-13).*

Number the squares in this grid with a marker, starting at one and going up in order. Place a rat into the box and observe its activity. Record the sequence of numbers of each square it enters. Does the rat show a preference for a particular part of the box as it moves about?

Projects With Preserved Materials

Preserved materials can come in many forms: insects neatly pinned in rows, study skins stored in museum cabinets, or fish and reptiles preserved in jars of alcohol. Zoologists collect and preserve these specimens for a variety of reasons. For example, preserved specimens can be used to help identify new forms of animals. Once identified, these preserved specimens can be used as a reference "library" for matching and identifying unknown specimens. Scientists can also gather evidence of evolutionary relationships by analyzing preserved zoological material.

The materials that zoologists preserve also sometimes can serve as bioindicators of pollution of the environment. For example, some zoologists study preserved materials in an attempt to find evidence of pollutants and contaminants like heavy metals and PCBs.

The study of preserved zoological specimens can tell a zoologist many things, including what a specific animal has eaten. The zoologist then has the opportunity to compare the diet of this animal with other species found within the same habitat.

Field biologists sometimes collect and preserve many individuals of a species being studied. These "voucher" specimens are used for the official identification of organisms being studied in the field.

In many cases, these organisms collected in the field

cannot be examined and identified immediately. The laboratory analysis of these animals can be very time-consuming. By preserving the organisms in alcohol or formalin, the zoologist has the opportunity to examine the animal at a later time under better conditions.

Biologists also preserve zoological specimens for use in teaching collections. By studying preserved specimens, students can learn much more about the morphology of the animal. Soft-bodied animals preserved in fluids remain soft and pliable for dissection or external examination.

Zoologists use two basic methods for preserving specimens for future study. The dry method of preservation can be used for hard-bodied invertebrates, such as insects and spiders, and for animal skins, skulls, teeth, and bones. It is important that specimens preserved by the dry method be stored in dark, dry places and that they be kept dust-free.

The wet preservation technique involves storing specimens in alcohol or formalin. You may have seen laboratory or museum specimens in jars that have been preserved by this method. Wet preservation is most suitable for fish, reptiles, amphibians, and whole animals (like worms and other soft-bodied invertebrates). It is also useful for preserving the internal organs of large animals. An advantage of the wet method of preservation is that, if done properly, there is no risk that the specimens will be damaged by pests or mold.

In the following projects, you will learn how to preserve insects in a collection, how to clean and preserve animal bones, and how to dissect an insect.

PROJECT 6-1: MAKING AN INSECT COLLECTION

Overview • It is not necessary to make a permanent collection to learn about insects. You can learn a great deal by studying insects in the field, by reading about them in field guides and other reference books, and by studying specimens exhibited in museums and nature centers. However, a collection with good data can be very valuable and may contribute important information and specimens in years to come. The material you collect and document may help biologists in future generations learn about environmental trends and changes.

The computerization of data has allowed museum and university entomologists around the world to share information collected by both amateur and professional zoologists. By pooling and analyzing this information and the collected specimens, these biologists are able to learn more about the environment and about the insects themselves. For example, the habitat in which an insect was collected may later be altered or destroyed. Preserved specimens may be the only record of organisms that once lived there.

No matter how large or small your insect collection, it should be carefully planned and cared for. Ask yourself why you are making the collection, what you plan to collect, and how you will care for it in years to come. All aspects of the collection procedure, from collecting to pinning to labeling, should be of museum quality.

Dispatching Insects • In the past, the most common method of killing, or dispatching, insects was to place them in a killing jar with a small amount of ethyl acetate, carbon tetrachloride, or other poison.

However, because of environmental and safety concerns, many entomologists now recommend the process of freezing specimens to avoid using toxic substances. After the specimens have been collected, they can be transported home or to the lab in plastic zip-lock bags or paper envelopes (which are used for butterflies, moths, and related insects). The specimens are then carefully placed into a part of the freezer where they will not be damaged.

If possible, leave the specimens in the freezer until you are ready to pin them into your permanent collection. If the insects are allowed to dry out after being removed from the freezer, they may become brittle and difficult to mount. If it is not possible to pin the insects immediately, place them in a "relaxing box" to soften the bodies of the insects. By "relaxing" the bodies, you can minimize damage to your specimens and make pinning much easier.

Using a Relaxing Box • You can use a refrigerator box with a snap-on lid for your relaxing box. Place a layer of moistened aquarium gravel on the bottom of the box. Cover the gravel with a piece of plastic screening, and carefully lay the specimens on top of the screen. You may wish to add a small amount of ascorbic acid to the water, before moistening the gravel, to prevent molding. Many biological supply companies also sell fast-acting relaxing fluid, which is marketed specifically for this purpose.

Pinning the Specimens • Most insects are preserved by a process called pinning. Special insect pins, which are longer and thinner than a regular stick pin, can be purchased from some scientific supply companies and hobby stores.

Carefully hold the insect between your thumb and forefinger, and insert the pin with your other hand. It is best to pin the insect as soon as possible after it is dispatched. Beetles are pinned through the right wing cover, while true bugs are pinned through the thorax. About one-fourth of the stainless steel entomological pin should project above the body of the insect.

Insects like butterflies and moths should be preserved with their wings spread. A spreading board can be made using cardboard or polystyrene (Figure 6-1). Pin the butterfly through the thorax from above, and place it at the standard height on the pin. Insert the

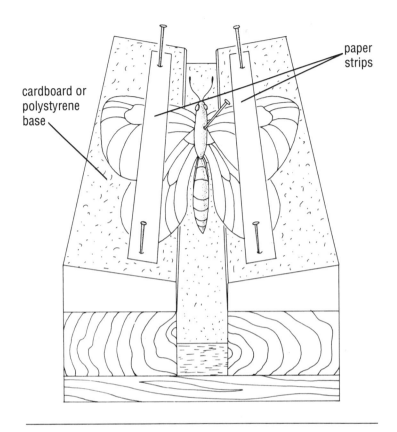

Figure 6-1. A spreading board is used to preserve butterflies and moths.

pin into the groove so that the base of the wings is even with the upper surface of the board. Carefully push the butterfly's or moth's wings open and down into position. Hold the wings in place with paper strips pinned to the board. Leave the wings in this position for about a week until they are dry.

Some insects, like leafhoppers and many flies, are so tiny that they would be almost impossible to pin. Instead, these small insects are lightly glued onto the tip of a small triangular white card, which is then pinned into place in the collection (see Figure 6-2). You can purchase special punches to make these triangular cards, or cut them yourself out of unruled index cards.

Labeling the Specimens • Label each specimen you collect with two small labels. The top label identifies the insect (using its scientific name), while the lower records the location and time of capture, as well as the collector's name. Additional information—such as weather, environmental conditions, or time of day—should be recorded in your ever-present notebook.

To help evenly space your labels, you can purchase a simple step block. You place the labels onto the block, and then push the pin through the hole. The step block will help give your collection a neat and uniform appearance.

It is important to choose a labeling style and to be consistent. Some abbreviations may be used, as long as they are consistent and a key (to the abbreviation) is provided.

Storing and Maintaining Your Collection • Your insect collection should be housed in a flat and airtight case, preferably one that is wooden. Insect cases can be purchased from most biological supply companies, but you may prefer to make your own display case, fronted by a large piece of glass. Weather stripping or another seal can be used to keep out dust, as well as to protect your collection from live insects that might try to feed on the specimens. The bottom of the case should be lined with white cardboard over a thin layer of cork or polystyrene, into which the pins are placed.

Some entomologists also put mothballs or flakes in a corner of the case (and secured with pins) to repel dermestid beetles, which can seriously damage or even destroy an unprotected collection. Since moth crystals

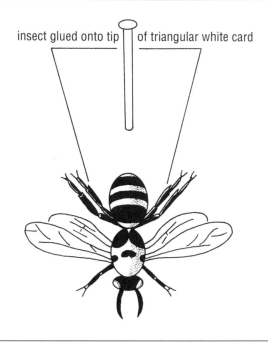

insect glued onto tip | | of triangular white card

Figure 6-2. Display tiny insects by gluing them lightly to triangular cards.

can interact with some materials, such as styrene, you may wish to enclose them in a small perforated box.

Butterflies and moths can be stored for years in triangular paper envelopes. It is important, of course, that all necessary field data be recorded on the envelope for future study. Natural history museums often have tens or hundreds of thousands of specimens stored this way.

Wet Preservation of Soft-Bodied Insects • Soft-bodied organisms, like the larval and nymph forms of many insects, can be preserved in small, tightly capped glass vials with 70 percent alcohol solution (seven parts alcohol to three parts distilled water). A small label should be placed inside each vial to identify the contents. Be sure to record the information with a marker or pencil that will not be affected by the alcohol solution.

PROJECT 6-2: PRESERVING AND STUDYING ANIMAL BONES

Overview • There are several reasons why zoologists preserve animal skeletons. The zoologist may use the skeletons and individual bones in research, perhaps to learn more about the animal's anatomy or relationship to other organisms. Skeletal mounts are also used as teaching tools in universities and museums. Bones can also be used as clues to an animal's identity or behavior.

In most natural history museums or nature centers, the skeletons on display are only a very small part of the museum's collection. Many more skeletons, individual bones, and bone fragments are stored "behind-the-scenes," where they are used for research.

You may find skeletons or bones as you explore the out-of-doors. If you wish to keep these bones for future study, you should clean them by following some basic procedures.

Zoologists often use insects as a biological method of cleaning skeletons. The bones are placed in a container with a large number of larvae of dermestid beetles. These beetles will eat the meat off of the bones. Bones can also be boiled to remove any residual meat. However, this is often a very smelly procedure, and one that you may wish to avoid. Zoologists also use forceps to remove any flesh remaining on the bones. Whatever method is used, it is important to wash your hands with a disinfectant soap after handling the bones.

After the bones are cleaned, they can be bleached by immersing them in hydrogen peroxide or household bleach **(caution)**.

PROJECT 6-3: DISSECTING AN INSECT

Overview • By dissecting an organism, a zoologist can learn about the internal structure of the animal, and also more about the environment and the animal's ecological role. For example, a zoologist could learn about harmful pollutants by analyzing the stomach or other tissue of an animal that has died.

Before doing a dissection, take the time to research the organism you are studying. By reading what other zoologists have learned, you may decide that a dissection is not necessary. As with any scientific research, you should define the objective for performing the investigation. Dissections should only be performed when they are necessary to learn more about the organism.

A standard dissecting kit includes instruments used not only for dissections, but also for the general handling of small organisms. A scissors and scalpel are included for cutting; however, you may prefer to use a small X-acto® or similar knife with a disposable blade. Thin, pointed probes are used for separating different parts of the specimen, and for lifting delicate organisms. Forceps, pins, and a dropper are also usually included. You can purchase a dissecting kit from most biological suppliers, or assemble one of your own.

You can make your own dissecting tray by pouring melted paraffin into a small metal pan. Use enough paraffin to form a layer of wax about one centimeter deep. This waxy bottom provides a good surface for inserting pins, which will hold the organism in position.

The following project gives you directions on how to dissect a cockroach. The cockroach is a good insect to dissect if you wish to learn more about the basic organs found in most insects. You can purchase a cockroach for this investigation from a biological supply company, as listed in the appendix of this book, or collect one yourself for dissection. Other large insects, like lubber grasshoppers, are also available from supply houses and are equally suitable for dissection.

Before performing the dissection, thoroughly examine the external morphology of the cockroach. Note the cockroach's hard, jointed exoskeleton. The exoskeleton consists of hard plates called sclerites, which are joined together by membranes for movement. Like all other insects, the cockroach has three main body regions: head, thorax, and abdomen.

The cockroach's two compound eyes are located on each side of its head. Two of its three smaller simple eyes (called ocelli) are visible as white ovals above the inner, upper margin of the compound eyes.

Use a probe to carefully open the cockroach's mouth. Then separate the various mouthparts with a forceps or probe. Examine each mouthpart and try to identify it. Can you find the triangular-shaped mandibles located under the upper lip? The mandibles are used for chewing, and move laterally (from side to side) within the cockroach's mouth. If you remove the mandibles you can find a second pair of jaws, called the maxillae. The maxillae are used for grasping and handling food.

The cockroach's thorax is the center of locomotion. Notice the two pairs of wings and three pairs of jointed legs. The fleshy pads on the surface of the cockroach's feet are used for gripping.

The cockroach's abdomen consists of eleven segments. If the cockroach you are examining is a female, you may be able to find the ovipositor.

Cockroaches are believed to be one of the oldest types of winged insects, dating back to perhaps more than 350 million years. They are extremely resilient and

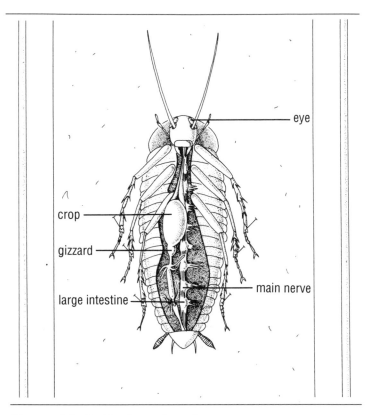

Figure 6-3. *Inside the cockroach*

resourceful, with flattened bodies that enable them to slip into narrow spaces. Figure 6-3 shows a view of a dissected cockroach.

Materials

dissecting tray	probe
scalpel or X-acto® knife	hand lens
forceps	cockroach
pins	salt water

Procedure

1. Examine the external morphology of the cockroach as described in the Overview to this project.
2. Position the cockroach on its back in your dissecting tray. Hold out and secure the legs with pins, and cover the insect with salt water.
3. Carefully cut up the midline of the cockroach's body. Pull back and examine the body casing, and pin it to the side of the body. Locate and lift up the gizzard, which is the short, rounded region at the end of the crop. The gizzard crushes and strains food before it passes into the intestines.
4. Carefully unravel the cockroach's coiled intestines, and find the nerve that runs down the back of the cockroach.

Further Investigations

1. Compare the anatomy of the cockroach with another insect (such as a grasshopper). Which organs and morphological features are the same? Which are different?

Appendix: Biological Supply Companies

Many of these companies will furnish a catalogue free of charge upon request. However, some large companies will only sell to organizations (like schools) that have purchase orders.

Therefore, you may find local sources of biological supplies that may be more convenient for you. You may wish to ask your science or biology teacher for nearby sources of the materials that you will need for your investigations.

American Biological Supply Company
1330 Dillon Heights
Baltimore, MD 21228

Carolina Biological Supply Company
2700 York Road
Burlington, NC 27215

Connecticut Valley Biological Supply Company
82 Valley Road
South Hampton, MA 01073

Edmund Scientific Company
101 E. Gloucester Pike
Barrington, NY 08007

Fisher Scientific Company
4901 W. LeMoyne Street
Chicago, IL 60651

Nasco
901 Janesville Avenue
Fort Atkinson, WI 53538

Sargent-Welch Scientific Company
7300 N. Linder
Skokie, IL 60077

Turtox/Cambrosco
8200 South Hoyne Avenue
Chicago, IL 60620

Ward's Natural Science Establishment, Inc.
5100 West Henrietta Road, Box 92912
Rochester, NY 14692

Glossary

abdomen: the posterior of the three major sections of an insect's body

anus: opening at the end of the digestive system, through which wastes are excreted

arachnid: an arthropod that has four pairs of legs

arthropod: any member of a group of invertebrates having segmented bodies, antennae, and paired and jointed legs

budding: a form of asexual reproduction, in which a group of cells breaks off the organism to form a new animal

caffeine: a common stimulant found in coffee, cola, and some other beverages

capillaries: tiny blood vessels in which nutrients and wastes are exchanged

carapace: the shieldlike covering of a crustacean

class: subdivision of a phylum, made up of a number of orders

clitellum: the enlarged section around the middle of the earthworm's body, which is used in reproduction

coelenterate: any member of a phylum of aquatic invertebrates that have two layers of tissue, ectoderm and endoderm, and a central body cavity; the three main groups of coelenterates are hydras, jellyfish, and corals and sea anemones *colony:* a group of a single species that lives cooperatively

community: group of populations that live in the same area and depend on each other for food

complete metamorphosis: metamorphosis with four distinct stages: egg, larva, pupa, and adult

compound microscope: a microscope with more than one power of magnification

control: the part of an experiment that does not receive the variable factor

crustacean: an arthropod that has two pairs of antennae and a hard exoskeleton

cryptozoa: the collective assembly of arthropods and other small animals found in leaf litter or soil

decomposer: an organism that helps to break down and recycle waste and dead organisms

dissect: to cut apart or separate for detailed examination

diurnal: related to or active during the daytime

dorsal: located on or related to the back of an animal

ecology: the study of organisms in relation to their surroundings

ectodermis: the layer of tissue that covers and protects the outside of an animal's body, such as a coelenterate

endodermis: the layer of tissue lining the body of an animal

entomology: the study of insects

formicarium: an artificial home for ants

genus: subdivision of a family, made up of numerous species

gizzard: an organ with heavy, muscular walls for grinding up food

herpetology: the study of reptiles and amphibians

home range: the area an animal occupies in the course of its daily activities

hypothesis: an unproven idea, used in science as a basis for further investigation *incomplete metamorphosis:* metamorphosis with immature forms called nymphs, which resemble the adults; nymphs develop wings and sexual organs

invertebrate: any animal without a backbone

isopod: any member of an order of crustaceans that have seven thoracic segments each carrying a pair of walking legs

larva: an immature stage of insects that undergo complete metamorphosis

mandibles: a pair of insect mouthparts that are used for chewing

molt: the shedding of the rigid cuticle to allow for growth or metamorphosis

morphology: the study of form and structure of an organism

nocturnal: active during the night

nymph: the immature form of insects, between the egg and adult, of species that undergo incomplete metamorphosis; nymphs resemble the adult form, and eat the same food as the adults

order: a subdivision of a class, made up of a number of families

orientation: the manner in which organisms position themselves in response to a stimulus, such as light

organism: an individual living thing

ornithology: the study of birds

ovipositor: the egg-laying appendage at the posterior of female insects

phylum: subdivision of a kingdom; a phylum is made up of classes

plankton: tiny, free-floating aquatic organisms

proboscis: a projecting mouthpart or snout, such as the tubelike sucking mouthpart of a fly or butterfly

pupa: stage of an insect between larva and adult in an insect that undergoes complete metamorphosis

respiration: the process of taking in oxygen and giving off carbon dioxide

sclerite: one of the hardened plates that compose the exoskeleton of an insect

setae: hairlike sensory structures that may be adapted to detect smell, taste, touch, or sound

social insects: species that live cooperatively in colonies, with a division of labor and distinct castes

tentacle: long flexible structures usually found around the mouth or head of some animals, like the hydra

territory: the portion of an animal's home range that is actively defended against other animals of its kind

thorax: the middle section of an insect's body, to which all legs and wings are attached

variable: the part of an experiment that is subject to change

ventral: located on or relating to the lower surface of an animal

vertebrate: an animal that has a backbone

For
Further
Reading

FIELD GUIDES

Covell, Charles. *Peterson Field Guide to Moths.* Boston: Houghton Mifflin, 1984.

Cox, Gerald. *Pond Life.* New York: M. Kesand, 1988.

Klots, Alexander. *Peterson Field Guide to Butterflies.* Boston: Houghton Mifflin, 1951.

Leahy, Chris. *Peterson First Guide to Insects.* Boston: Houghton Mifflin, 1987.

Levi, Herbert. *Spiders and Their Kin.* New York: Golden Press, 1987.

Milne, L. and M. *The Audubon Society Field Guide to North American Insects and Spiders.* New York: Alfred Knopf, 1980.

Murie, Olaus. *Peterson Field Guide to Animal Tracks.* Boston: Houghton Mifflin, 1974.

Peterson, Roger T. *Field Guide to Birds.* Boston: Houghton Mifflin, 1980.

Pyle, Robert. *The Audubon Society Field Guide to North American Butterflies.* New York: Alfred A. Knopf, 1981.

Reid, George. *Pond Life: A Guide to Common Plants and Animals of North American Ponds and Lakes.* New York: Golden Press, 1987.

Zim, Herbert, and C. Cottom. *Insects.* New York: Golden Press, 1987.

Bochinski, Julianne Blair. *The Complete Handbook of Science Fair Projects.* New York: John Wiley & Sons, 1991.

Durrell, Gerald. *The Amateur Naturalist.* New York: Alfred A. Knopf, 1982.

Focus on Life Science. Columbus, OH: Merrill Publishing Company, 1989.

Globe Biology. Englewood Cliffs, NJ: Globe Book Company, 1990.

Imes, Rick. *The Practical Entomologist.* New York: Simon & Schuster, 1992.

MacFarlane, Ruth E. *Making Your Own Nature Museum.* New York: Franklin Watts, 1989.

Pringle, Laurence. *Discovering Nature Indoors.* New York: Natural History Press, 1970.

Rainis, Kenneth. *Nature Projects for Young Scientists.* New York: Franklin Watts, 1989.

Roth, Charles E. *The Amateur Naturalist.* New York: Franklin Watts, 1993.

Russo, Monica. *The Insect Almanac.* New York: Sterling Publishing Company, 1991.

Tocci, Salvatore. *Biology Projects for Young Scientists.* New York: Franklin Watts, 1986.

Index

(Page numbers in *italics* refer to illustrations.)

About The Author

Mary Dykstra received a B.S. in education from Carroll College in Waukesha, Wisconsin, with an emphasis in environmental studies. She later completed an internship at the Manomet Bird Observatory in Massachusetts, where she assisted with passerine banding, research, and educational outreach programs. Her experience in educational program development has included stints as an environmental education specialist and middle school science teacher. While on the staff of the Milwaukee Public Museum, she developed educational programs and materials, and conducted teacher workshops in conjunction with a local university. Ms. Dykstra has made numerous trips to Central America, where she has assisted with field studies in the rain forest of Costa Rica. She enjoys bird-watching and hiking in her home state of Wisconsin.